THE
Encouragers

THE Encouragers

Discovering your
ministry of affirmation

JEANNE DOERING

CHRISTIAN HERALD BOOKS
Chappaqua, New York

Unless otherwise indicated, all Scripture quotations are from *The New American Standard Bible*, © The Lockman Foundation, 1960, 1962, 1968, 1971, 1972, 1973, 1975. Used by permission.

Verses marked TLB are from *The Living Bible*, copyright 1971 by Tyndale House Publishers, Wheaton, Ill. Used by permission.

Verses marked NIV are from the *Holy Bible: New International Version*, copyright © by the New York International Bible Society. Used by permission of Zondervan Bible Publishers.

Verses marked Amplified are from *The Amplified New Testament*, © 1954, 1958 The Lockman Foundation. Used by permission.

Portions from "Touch: New Dimension of Faith," by L. Arden Almquist, reprinted by permission from *Christian Life Magazine*, copyright November 1969, Christian Life Inc., 396 E. St. Charles Road, Wheaton, Ill. 60187.

Excerpt from "New Year, 1945" reprinted with permission of Macmillan Publishing Co., Inc., from *The Cost of Discipleship*, 2nd Edn., by Dietrich Bonhoeffer, ©SCM Press Ltd., 1959.

Quotations from *Life Together* by Dietrich Bonhoeffer, trans. John Doberstein, reprinted by permission of Harper and Row Publishers, Inc., © 1954.

"Manuscript Reader's Prayer" by Walter MacPeek from *The Journalist's Prayer Book*, copyright 1972, Augsburg Publishing House. Used by permission.

Library of Congress Cataloging in Publication Data

Doering. Jeanne I.
  The encouragers.
  Includes bibliographical references.
  1. Lay ministry. 2. Encouragement. 3. Helping behavior. I. Title
BV677.D63   253.5   81-68641   ISBN 0-86693-004-3   AACR2

MEMBER OF
EVANGELICAL CHRISTIAN
PUBLISHERS ASSOCIATION

Christian Herald, independent, evangelical and interdenominational, is dedicated to publishing wholesome, inspirational and religious books for Christian families.

First Edition
CHRISTIAN HERALD BOOKS, 40 Overlook Drive, Chappaqua, New York 10514
Printed in the United States of America

*To Mom and Dad,
who encouraged me
before Jesus called
them both Home
in 1978*

Acknowledgments

If you're reading this page, you have something in common with me. While most people pass up acknowledgments as a book's deadwood, I often find myself reading them. I like to know who inspired the author and kept him going.

I am indebted to:

Harry Albus. In the fall of 1979 I visited Harry and his wife in Portland, Oregon. I told them about a little free-lance article I was doing on "The Barnabas Committee." By the end of the evening, Harry was telling me, "You ought to write a book on encouragement." And this was from a man who had written books himself.

Dr. Glenn Arnold. He was my professor and advisor at Wheaton Graduate School and guided me through the first version of this—my master's thesis.

Helen Elliot. This Wycliffe Bible translator, serving in Guatemala, graciously told me about incidents of encouragement from her life and gave helpful suggestions for the first draft.

Pastors I have known. Men such as Hilton Jarvis, Chuck Swindoll, Ron Eggert, Don Knapp, Kent Hughes, and Dave Gotaas helped build Scriptures into my life.

People who prayed. Ones like "Grandma G"—Halcyon Gillespie; friends at Family Bible Fellowship, Puyallup, Washington; and others demonstrated "the community of encouragement."

Jeanne Doering
Chicago, 1981

Psalm 115:1

Contents

PART I
The Nature of Encouragement

The Barnabas Committee

For [Barnabas] was a good man, and full of the Holy Spirit and of faith. —Luke, the physician (Acts 11:24)

I went to college in the sixties with the "Generation of the Discontented." Ad hoc committees of all sorts festered in various campus wounds. If they didn't like curfew at the student center, then it was the grading system. Or an administrator's style. The selection of ice cream flavors. Certain companies that recruited on campus.

The negative atmosphere bothered me. I was glad to get my diploma—and get out.

But when I started working I found much of the same. Instead of carrying signs, having sit-ins, or writing angry letters to editors, the ad hoc committees muttered at coffee breaks or lunch. If it wasn't the pay scale, then it was so-and-so who owed his job only to Uncle Elmer. Or the guys in such-and-such department who didn't have brains to tie their shoes.

After several years of working, I took a one-year cram course at a Bible college. I thought studying the Bible all day would be heaven on earth.

But negatives crept in with the first autumn drizzles. My study load far exceeded the available hours. Two roommates had boyfriend traumas. Another was homesick. I signed up for voice lessons and came down with a string of sore throats.

My car coughed to death at intersections. The battery rattled its finale and then slept in peace. My bank account developed a chronic leak.

Letters from home told of my dad's despair and aimlessness after the company forced him into an early retirement. Mother's too-regular cancer checkups concerned me. Then she broke her leg.

The gloomies hit other students, too. Talk at meals and prayer cells became a contest of whose problem was the worst. Many professors battled sickness and uncertainties. Finances and a drop in enrollment worried the administration.

It seemed the Author of Discouragement was having a heyday. I could imagine C.S. Lewis's "Uncle Screwtape" gleefully penning his junior temptor Wormwood, "You are marvelously distracting these Bible school humans from the purposes of our Enemy. Well done, thou bad and faithful nephew."

Then one chilly morning a first period class in the gospels changed my life and outlook. The professor was a rookie—fresh out of seminary—and struggling to keep up with lesson preparations in unfamiliar territory. Many times as I walked home at night from the library I saw his office light on and his head bent over the books.

After the bell, he paused and, instead of starting the lecture, asked for our understanding and forgiveness for his poor preparation over the past few weeks. He requested our prayers for his overwhelming work load. I noticed his hands were shaking as he put on his glasses and then started the lecture.

The class was stunned.

I was prodded to do something—positive.

Over the next few days "The Barnabas Committee" was born. A handful of other students and I committed ourselves to pray for and encourage this professor and other faculty and staff.

We decided to remain anonymous to avoid embarrassment and charges of seeking favoritism. But we also wanted to communicate our concern and love.

Our solution? Little typed notes of encouragement, sometimes in silly rhymes, with attached gifts such as candy bars, apples, or animal crackers. We sent these encouragement parcels (signed, "The Barnabas Committee") through the campus mail or sneaked around campus at night to deliver them at office doors.

We weren't prepared for the reaction. Many sent the committee thank-you notes in care of the campus post office. But the clerk didn't know where to deliver them. Finally these thank-yous found a home in the school bulletin between classroom changes and soccer practice times.

When the committee left a May basket of suckers for the weekly faculty meeting, this gem followed.

Each one of us, dear Barnabas,
Finds our vest buttons hopping,
Not only for the pride of you,
But calories—lolli-popping.
Our "pulchritude," our "attitude,"
Our "fortitude," our tickers,
Were touched, enhanced and blessed
By your bag full of lickers.

—The Faculty

In a way we never expected, the message was out to the whole campus: "Encourage one another." We noticed others starting to do similar things. People responded with lifted spirits. The campus mood turned positive.

And the amazing thing was this: as we concentrated on encouraging other people, we were encouraged ourselves.

Graduation brought an end to the Barnabas Committee's nocturnal ministry. At commencement, as I walked across the platform with my new diploma, I stifled the urge to wink at those profs whom I'd helped to "encourage."

Lesson two on encouragement

Little did I know, however, how soon God would enroll me in an advanced course on encouragement. Nor how deeply those lessons would hurt and cost.

The advanced course began a year later, in 1978, with phone calls that shook my world apart and left me, like an earthquake victim, weeping over the rubble.

The first phone call came at work one June morning in Portland, Oregon. The call was from Dad. Mother was in the hospital and probably wouldn't last the night. "Come quickly," he pleaded.

My courage collapsed. Yet somehow on that chilled, rainy, dreary day I found the strength to drive into the next state and locate the hospital.

Mother was already unconscious. We waited, holding her hands. For twelve hours we watched her gasp and groan. The nurses came in, gently checked her pulse and i.v.s, injected more pain relievers, dabbed her cracked lips with moisture, squeezed our shoulders, and silently left.

Early the next morning she died. I hurt for her suffering, for my own loss. But my heart was broken more in seeing my dad's devastation. I didn't know how to comfort him. I could only hug him and say words that seemed too empty.

Now a heavy decision pressed my heart. In another two months I had planned to start graduate studies in Illinois, far away from "home" in Washington state. Seeing my father's great grief, his listlessness, his confusion over what to do with Mother's things, I wondered if I should abandon those plans, find some type of job near home (though it wouldn't be in my field) and live with Dad while he worked through his grief.

But close friends and the family urged me to go ahead and start graduate school. So, late in August, I packed my clothes and typewriter into the car and left. For the first hour of driving I could hardly see road signs for tears; my arms still felt the heaviness of Dad's good-bye embrace.

As I struggled with graduate work, Dad's needs loomed ever before me. I wrote him at least a post card once or twice a week. I called a few times but he choked up and found it difficult to talk. I didn't know how else to encourage him.

Then came that second phone call the second week of my second quarter in school. My daddy was dead of a heart attack. He had survived Mother by only six months.

For me, life could no longer go on the same way. As the single and "available" daughter, I felt I had no choice but to drop out of school and go back to Washington to empty out the family home and settle legal affairs. I was old enough to be on my own (as I had been for years), but I was crushed, painfully aware of my new status as an orphan.

I dipped into my school savings for living expenses while I spent all my time sorting through their belongings, holding garage sales, and painting up the house so it would sell better. I desperately wanted to finish the task as quickly as possible. I knew there was nothing permanent for me "at home" any more.

Although the family house was not strange to me, everything else was. I had lived in six other cities since high school. Here I had no deep roots and no church home. I knew only a handful of my parents' friends—and then just barely.

I wanted to be brave, to be an example to others of the strength that Jesus Christ can give to handle grief and discouragement. But as the months dragged on I realized that I was starved for affirmation, for encouragement, for consolation.

At times I wondered if there would ever be a way out of my circumstances. I doubted my self-worth. I almost asked why I was cluttering up the world. My sister was busy with two children and the business she and her husband had started. They had many demands on them and good reasons to live. But I found myself asking, What about me? Am I really needed? Some days were incredibly black.

At times only my commitment to clean out and sell the house and honorably finish the probate task kept me going. As I look back, I know people stepped in to encourage me. But my needs were so deep that often I felt only isolation and emptiness.

Discovering biblical encouragers

My hurt drove me to search the Bible for special encouragement from God. He showed me many who had found His consolation and passed it on to others. My too-theological concept of encouragement changed and came to life. Instead of regarding it as just a "spiritual gift" that only some have (Rom. 12:8), I saw how threads of caring run liberally throughout the whole fabric of Scripture.

I realized that encouragement involved many "gifts" or special, Spirit-endowed abilities; many techniques; and above all a living, growing faith within a living, growing Body—the church. I had to agree with the martyred German pastor Dietrich Bonhoeffer:

> Do we really think there is a single person in this world who does not need either encouragement or admonition? Why, then, has God bestowed Christian brotherhood on us?[1]

I saw how we need to encourage one another because our sin-tainted world delights in discouragement. Negative people can pollute our outlooks; negative circumstances, our hope. These can easily strangle our spiritual lives unless we are at work encouraging one another. As Hebrews 3:13 warns believers,

> But encourage one another day after day, as long as it is still called "Today," lest any one of you be hardened by the deceitfulness of sin.

I realized our Barnabas Committee had touched a hot wire when we identified with one of the New Testament's largely unsung heroes. Really a Levite from Cyprus named Joseph, the apostles, perhaps for a dominant personality trait, tagged him "Barnabas," which means "Son of Consolation" or "Son of Encouragement." What a generous label! Just imagine being called "Encourager"!

I wondered if Barnabas was a big, strong, likable type with a healthy "holy hug"—something like a good-humored Dutch farmer. Certain Scriptures hint that he may have been a large man. When he and Paul went to Lystra on the first missionary journey, the local people mistook them for gods. They hailed the articulate Paul as Hermes (a god who conveyed messages for other gods), then named Barnabas after thunder-throated Zeus (their most prominent deity). Perhaps he looked the part.

His physique is speculation. But Scripture unmistakably portrays him as a caring and giving man—giving not only out of his pocketbook (as he did when we first meet him in Acts) but also out of his heart. In private and in public, his counsel and consolation helped heal the hurting.

I saw several things in Barnabas's life that characterize the Christian encourager.

First, he tapped into God's resources. Scripture's thumbnail sketch of him says, "For Barnabas was a good man, and full of the Holy Spirit and of faith" (Acts 11:24). I like how this is expressed by the Amplified version:

> For he was a good man [good in himself and also at once for the good and the advantage of other people], full of and controlled by the Holy Spirit and full of faith [that is, of his belief that Jesus is the Messiah, through Whom we obtain eternal salvation].

Barnabas had received Jesus Christ as his Messiah and personal Savior from sin and had been empowered by the Holy Spirit to serve others. There's no way he could have done all that he did without the resources of Someone greater than himself.

To "draw alongside"

Second, as the Lord's vessel of service, he made himself available to "draw alongside." That is the literal meaning of the Greek word *parakletos* which means "encourager." The same word is used in John 15 to describe the Holy Spirit as the "Comforter." Barnabas knew how to approach and help people in need.

When I think of "coming alongside," I recall the hot August afternoon that a college student struggled with a heavy suitcase, pillow, bulging book bag, and purse as she tried to walk to the train depot about a mile away. Repeatedly, she dropped one thing and then another as her frustration built.

Another student happened to look up from her studies and saw the struggling traveler. She remembered the train was due at the station in less than ten minutes. The girl with the suitcase would never make it. She burst out of her apartment and ran to meet her.

"Are you headed to the train?" she asked as she took the pillow and book bag. They ran together the remaining blocks and arrived just as the train whistled up.

Someone was helped because someone else saw a need and came alongside with a solution. That's encouragement.

In his second appearance in Acts, Barnabas came alongside someone who was a religious outcast. The man's name was Saul and nobody trusted him. A short time before he had been killing Christians. Now he was back in town a changed man, telling people of his conversion to Christianity.

The apostles were skeptical. Perhaps Saul had gone mad—or was spying on them. But Barnabas stopped to listen and to hear Saul out. He sensed potential in somebody that everyone else considered a misfit. Then he took Saul back to the apostles and retold Saul's testimony (Acts 9:27). This time they were more accepting and took Saul in.

A few years later, when Barnabas and Saul (renamed Paul) were a famous missionary team, Barnabas saw in his cousin John Mark another uncut gem, perhaps another Paul. He wanted to take the young man along on their second missionary journey. But Paul refused. John Mark had deserted them earlier and Paul didn't want to go through that again.

Neither would yield and they split. Paul left with Silas. Barnabas stuck with John Mark. The argument cost Barnabas a potentially famous role in helping Paul shape the New Testament church. But his decision to come alongside a kid labeled "coward" bore fruit. From that young man's pen came the gospel of Mark. Before Paul's death, the great apostle admitted that Mark had been useful in his ministry (2 Tim. 4:11).

Third, Barnabas was skilled as a communicator of encouragement. In a way that perfectly complemented his style of relating to people, God enabled him to affirm others and point their focus upward.

Barnabas's techniques

You might call what he practiced the "encouragement techniques" that this book will discuss. But I sincerely doubt that Barnabas stopped long enough to think about *how* he encouraged people. Out of the fullness of his walk with Jesus Christ, he simply poured himself out to help people.

Think of the challenge of counseling and affirming one-on-one that new Christian named Saul, or the balm that had to be rubbed into John Mark's wounded self-esteem.

Barnabas could also encourage and inspire large groups of people. When the Jerusalem church sent him to Antioch to check out rumors that Gentiles had become Christians, Acts 11:23 says "he rejoiced and began to encourage them all with resolute heart to remain true to the Lord."

Later, teamed with Paul and preaching in churches they had started in Asia Minor, Barnabas's ministry involved "strengthening the souls of the disciples, encouraging them to continue in the faith" (Acts 14:22). I think he must have given them a healthy dose of "future-tense encouragement," reminding them of their glorious future because of the Resurrection.

A servant's heart

Fourth, Barnabas had a servant heart, expecting no glory for his efforts. Look at his relationship with Paul. Shortly after his conversion, with his life in danger, Paul went home to Tarsus. But Barnabas didn't forget him. A few years later the Encourager tracked down Paul and brought him to Antioch where he discipled Paul into a powerful man of God.

Saul started to shine. Barnabas could have felt threatened, but there's no hint of that in Scripture. One clue to that is the order in which he and Paul are named in the accounts of their mission work. In Acts 11:30, it's "Barnabas and Saul" assigned to deliver a famine relief offering. In Acts 12:25 it's "Barnabas and Saul" returning from that task.

In Acts 13:1-2 he headed the list of potential missionary appointees, with Saul coming last. It's the same order when they went to Paphos and met the proconsul (Acts 13:7).

But that first missionary trip marked a change. After their work in Cyprus they sailed across the Mediterranean and started through Asia Minor. At Pisidian Antioch Paul preached the sermon that stirred up the city. Note Acts 13:42: "And as Paul and Barnabas were going out, the people kept begging that these things might be spoken to them the next Sabbath."

No longer was it "Barnabas and Paul." Paul took leadership and prominence. Throughout the rest of Acts, with only one exception (Acts 14:14), Paul had the distinction of being number one man. Paul was the soloist of their duet. As God blessed the ministry of Barnabas's junior partner, Barnabas didn't demand equal billing. He quietly stepped aside to let God do His work.

A similar thing happened with the famous London preacher F.B. Meyer, who annually came to America to preach. He always brought out the crowds and impressed the statisticians. But later in his life somebody named G. Campbell Morgan came on the scene. Meyer's faithfuls started to go hear Morgan instead.

What did Meyer do? He went to prayer and later was seen going about town saying: "Have you heard G. Campbell Morgan? God gifted him." The man who had known fame became a Barnabas and bowed out to let another star shine. There was no competition, only encouragement and a servant's heart.

Fifth, Barnabas disregarded the cost. Financially, encouraging cost him a tract of land, probably his security against some lean times. He also gave up going back to a comfortable career in Cyprus. Instead he spent his life tracking over scrubby hills, dodging stonings, and pouring his life into downcast people.

He illustrated an attitude that Paul would later put to words: "I count all things to be loss in view of the surpassing value of knowing Christ Jesus my Lord" (Phil. 3:8).

Giving is its own response

This is where most people fail as encouragers. They want results from their good deeds, recognition for their labors.

And why not? It's human to seek positive feedback for concern shown. When we pet a cat, we want it to purr.

But God's economy doesn't work on a tidy "in-go equals out-go" basis. The heroes of the faith in Hebrews 11, for example, persisted in their obedience to God, even though they never saw in this life what He had promised. And more than that, those of us who are Christians are the product of an impossibly lopsided equation. God's input certainly doesn't equal our outgo in producing salvation. We can offer nothing—not even nice-guy deeds or a plate piled with tithes—for our salvation in Jesus Christ. Calvary's price tag reads "priceless." Our part, put forth in faith, is zero. Yet it brings us God's infinity. We love and encourage—expecting nothing—because He first loved us, though we didn't deserve that love. Then we leave the results of our ministry love to God.

Books about great preaching are usually written by great preachers; those about great praying, by great men and women of prayer.

Although I am writing about encouragement, I am *not* a great encourager. There are aspects of this ministry in which I am terribly deficient. Some of my sensitivities to people are badly dulled by pride and self-pity. Encouragement has been a tough curriculum for me.

Thankfully, not all of it was completely new material. I learned that some things that I had always done came under the label of "encouragement." But I also saw how much more I could do.

My study showed me that encouragement involves two dimensions: horizontal and vertical.

The horizontal part takes place when we reach out to others who hurt and who need all that the word "encourage" implies. It requires sharpening our verbal and nonverbal communication skills. It demands being faithful in little things, giving without expecting return. In short, it means the Barnabas mindset.

But all the emotional and spiritual energy required by a ministry of encouragement will quickly drain away unless we are tuned into the vertical aspect of encouragement.

We learn about that through a man who (like me, many times!) despaired, collapsed under a desert broom tree, and sang the blues.

The Broom Tree Blues 2

If God sends us on stony paths, He provides strong shoes. —Corrie ten Boom[2]

I'm waiting for a Nashville type to come up with something called the "Broom Tree Blues."

The story? A cloudburst, a woman's jealousy, two marathon runs, an attempt to outwit the posse, and plain down-in-the-dumps depression at the end of the trail.

But it has a second ending, a good one and biblical. The lyrics come straight out of Elijah's ups-and-downs in 1 Kings 18 and 19.

What does this have to do with encouraging one another? It's this: Ministering encouragement requires victory over its opposite, discouragement.

Elijah didn't start out discouraged. He was going strong on a spiritual high. After watching God miraculously ignite the water-soaked altars at Mount Carmel, he defended God's honor by slaying the prophets of the false god Baal. Then when Elijah prayed for rain to break the three-year drought, the sky puckered up and dropped a flood.

Of course, somebody had to be unhappy about it. Humiliated instead of grateful, King Ahab the Baal-worshipper stomped into his chariot and bumped through the mud puddles as fast as he could home to Jezreel, twenty miles away.

Elijah, ecstatic over his spiritual victory and expecting others to be too, tucked his droopy robes into his belt, raced

Ahab's chariot on foot, and beat it to the finish line. He would have been a shoo-in for the Boston Marathon.

But Jezebel, Ahab's less-than-lovely wife, was in no mood to cheer this victor and rain-bringer. She sent Elijah a little note that said: "I'm going to have you killed."

First prick in that balloon called a spiritual high.

Elijah had to read the note only once to realize he had to get out of town—and fast. As 1 Kings 19:3 puts it, "He was afraid and arose and ran for his life and came to Beersheba, which belongs to Judah, and left his servant there."

Jezreel to Beersheba is eighty miles as the raven flies and even more as a lizard scampers. The Mount Carmel race was only a warmup next to Elijah's panicked run to Beersheba. But Elijah knew even Beersheba was no place to hang around—not with Jezebel's posse after him. He left his servant there and went another day's journey into the wilderness.

Finally, wiped out, he collapsed under a nearly leafless broom tree and asked God to let him die.

Discouragement in the raw.

While the desert sun beat down mercilessly, he probably pulled part of his robe over his head, closed his eyes, and hoped to wake up in heaven. Indeed, an angel woke him. But he blinked open his eyes and saw to his chagrin that he was still under a dusty old broom tree in the same old desert. He ached, he was dirty and sweaty, and he was hungry.

Then he heard, "Arise, eat."

He looked over and saw a little cake of bread and jar of water. Amazed, yet too hungry to think about it, he washed down huge bites, then curled up to sleep again.

After a while, the angelic room service knocked again. Another meal sat ready on the rocks. "Eat up," the angel said. "You've got a long trip ahead of you."

He left his broom tree and went down to the Sinai and into some of the most barren parts of the world. As he stumbled for forty days and nights over the blazing, lunar-like landscape, Elijah probably wondered why God was taking him so far away to die. Finally he came to Mount Horeb (where God had given Israel the Ten Commandments), spotted a cave, crawled in, and waited.

If anybody needed encouragement, it was Elijah. But there were no other creatures around, except maybe some sand fleas. Probably lots of self-pity swirled in his mind. Here he'd given up everything for God and done great works—for a hot cave in the middle of nowhere.

When God asked, "What are you doing here, Elijah?" the prophet had his answer well-rehearsed. He wiped some sweat off his face and whined: "I have been very zealous for the LORD, the God of hosts; for the sons of Israel have forsaken Thy covenant, torn down Thine altars and killed Thy prophets with the sword. And I alone am left; and they seek my life, to take it away" (1 Kings 19:10).

You don't sing lyrics like that to the tune "Happy Wanderer." If this was living for the Lord, Elijah wanted to drop out. He didn't have any friends left (so he thought) and now even God had let him down (so he concluded). His ministry to others had shriveled like a hundred-year pickle.

What Elijah didn't realize was that the trail into the desert would eventually lead to another mountain top. But along the way God had to take him aside to renew him with divine encouragement.

First, God attended to the physical source of Elijah's depression, giving him rest and good food.

Then, God gave the prophet a new glimpse of divine resources. To remind the prophet of His undiminished power and might, He dispatched a rock-splitting wind, then an incredible earthquake, and finally a fire. Next, God showed Elijah His loving gentleness in the soft wind through which He spoke.

Finally, God pushed Elijah out of the cave of self-pity and

sent him off on a new ministry to anoint two new kings and his own successor. Never again did Elijah croon "The Broom Tree Blues." Encouraged by God, he realized the power for his ministry had to come from divine sources—and would. He had experienced God's love, reaffirmed his faith, and set out again with hope.

I see a very similar message in a key New Testament passage that reminds us to encourage one another:

> Let us consider how to stimulate one another to love and good deeds, not forsaking our own assembling together, as is the habit of some, but encouraging *one another,* and all the more, as you see the day drawing near (Heb. 10:24-25).

Faith + love + hope = encouragement

The full meaning of these verses comes out through the five that precede them. They show how Christian encouragement requires faith *and* hope *and* love.

"Faith" is expressed in verses 19 through 22, which say we can "draw near [to God] with a sincere heart in full assurance of faith." Old Testament believers had to approach God through a system of sacrifices. But Hebrews teaches how Christ's death at Calvary did away with that system since He was the perfect, once-for-all sacrifice for sin.

"Hope" comes out of verse 23: "Let us hold fast the confession of our hope without wavering, for He who promised is faithful." Our faith leads to our hope, because of God's faithfulness demonstrated at Calvary. He sees—and will meet—our needs. I think one of David's psalms could easily apply to Elijah's "dessert" in the desert.

> The LORD sustains all who fall,
> And raises up all who are bowed down.
> The eyes of all look to Thee,

And Thou dost give them their food in due time.
Thou dost open Thy hand,
And dost satisfy the desire of every living thing
(Psalm 145:14-16).

Intimate knowledge of God's faithfulness prepares the encourager for his ministry. And often God chooses to allow us time in the deserts of trouble to humble us, purify us, and show us Himself.

The English preacher Charles Spurgeon, for example, learned that when depression forced him to go back to the promises of God's faithfulness, God was preparing him for something greater. "The cloud is black before it breaks," he wrote. "It overshadows before it yields its deluge of mercy. Depression has now become to me as a prophet in rough clothing, a John the Baptist heralding the nearer coming of my Lord's richer blessing."[3]

Black clouds of discouragement often shadowed another great man, missionary-to-China Hudson Taylor. Burdened by meager finances and personal grief (he buried his wife and some children in China), he persisted against strong resistance. He would often say: "It doesn't matter, really, how great the pressure is. It only matters where the pressure lies. See that it never comes between you and the Lord—then, the greater the pressure, the more it presses you to His breast."[4]

He looked to God's faithfulness. He had no time to pout under a broom tree—instead, he held fast the confession of his faith and didn't waver.

Finally, the outworking of our faith and hope is "love." The Amplified version expresses verse 24 of chapter 10 as follows:

> Let us consider and give attentive, continuous care to watching over one another, studying how we may stir up (stimulate and incite) to love and helpful deeds and noble activities.

This shows how encouragement is more than passing out "warm fuzzies." It's being caretakers of one another and being watchful of our Christian walk.

Encouragement's other side

If I were to describe a coin—say, a penny—I would have to tell about both sides. One pictures Lincoln's Memorial and the other shows Lincoln's head. Just because one side is different from the other does not make it any less a penny. The same is true of the Greek word *parakaleo*, which we often translate "encourage" in Scripture.

Most of us equate "encouraging" with "comforting," "consoling," "helping," or "heartening." It's that, but it's also "beseeching," "exhorting," and "calling forth." It's urging people to walk rightly, to "walk in a manner worthy of the Lord" (Col. 1:10).

It carries the idea of a loving watchfulness such as a father has over his children. Paul described that in his letter to the Thessalonians:

> You know how we were exhorting and encouraging and imploring each one of you as a father would his own children, so that you may walk in a manner worthy of the God who calls you into His own kingdom and glory (1 Thess. 2:11-12).

True love for the brethren is concerned with their spiritual welfare. And that must be done in the context of a worshipping community. Thus the writer to the Hebrews urged believers to get together regularly, "not forsaking our own assembling together, as is the habit of some, but encouraging one another" (10:25). When we come together we find out who is hurting. We can comfort. We can discern who is straying. We can exhort.

From God to us to others

When we are transparent with one another, the comfort or correction we receive may be the message God wants delivered later to another. During a church service I admitted my weakness in a certain area and asked for prayer. Afterwards someone came to me and said, "Thanks for asking prayer for that. I have the same problem. You have shown me that I need to ask the support of other Christians to conquer it."

But my willingness to admit my weaknesses—and an ability to tell about God's encouragement and faithfulness—didn't really come until He had led me through a spiritual desert.

I'm reminded of that every time I see two oil paintings by my parents which I hung over my living-room sofa. The one by my father shows a desert in hot, thirst-provoking oranges and reds. Although I'm fond of Western Washington's green blanket of forests and spine of ice-cream mountains, I've also learned to appreciate the desert of the eastern part of the state.

One time I stopped at a desert turnoff for a drowsy-driver break and ventured warily into the sands. One eye alert for snakes, I paused and listened. The little-used road was empty. There was only the whack of the incessant wind against my car and the whish of the sand, moving in gritty vapors from one corduroy ridge to another. The beauty was haunting.

When I found that desert painting by my dad in a closet a few months after my parents' deaths, I realized how my grief and the clean-up probate task had put my life in a spiritual desert—dry, gritty, barren. But I thought, too, of something I had just read in Deuteronomy.

He found him in a desert land,
And in the howling waste of a wilderness;

> He encircled him, He cared for him,
> He guarded him as the pupil of his eye (32:10).

Just as God had guarded Israel and later Elijah, so He would not abandon me in these deserts of discouragement. As Fanny Crosby wrote in that memorable hymn:

> He hideth my soul in the cleft of the rock
> That shadows a dry, thirsty land.
> He hideth my soul in the depths of his love,
> And covers me there with His hand.

Even in these howling wastes, God was there to cover me!

A similar message came from the other painting, one my mother completed just a couple of months before she died. It shows Mount Rainier mirrored in a lake at the summit of Chinook Pass. I often drove over that pass when I traveled between my parents' and sister's homes at opposite ends of the state.

I love watching the mountains, but on one of those trips, that lonely year after my parents' deaths, I was so discouraged that I barely noticed the scenery. Then I came to the summit of Chinook, and the white-robed giant suddenly rose in regal glory in front of me. Startled, I pulled the car to the side, yanked on the brake, and turned off the motor. I fumbled in my things for my Bible, then walked up to a rock where firs framed the mountain. I knew the psalm the Lord intended as as exhortation.

> I will lift up my eyes to the mountains;
> From whence shall my help come?
> My help comes from the LORD,
> Who made heaven and earth (Psalm 121:1-2).

As tears dribbled down my cheeks, I prayed my gratefulness for the massive reminder of encouragement before me. My help would come from the Lord, not from my own resources. Elijah had to learn that, and so did I.

As the day draws near

In the barren places, God encourages us. In response, we are to encourage others. And we are to do this, according to Hebrews 10:25, "all the more, as you see the day drawing near." "The day," of course, refers to the coming of the Lord. Hebrews was written probably a year or two before the fall of Jerusalem and many believed the unrest they witnessed was leading to the cataclysmic event that would end the world and usher in the new age.

It didn't—God had a different timetable than they supposed. But prophecies from the full revelation of Scripture do suggest that *our* generation may be the one to witness the end of the world and the second coming of the Lord Jesus Christ. He urges us to be ready, "for you do not know which day your Lord is coming" (Matt. 24:42).

Being ready doesn't mean sitting around until everything falls apart. In one of His parables about the end times, Jesus said, "Blessed is that slave whom his master finds so doing [alert and at work] when he comes" (Matt. 24:46). That work includes the ministry of encouragement—and *all the more* as the Day of the Lord draws near. What Paul wrote to the Thessalonians is ever truer for us: "Encourage one another, and build up one another, just as you also are doing. . . . Admonish the unruly, encourage the fainthearted, help the weak, be patient with all men" (1 Thess. 5:11, 14).

Many Scriptures point out creative ways through which Christians can communicate encouragement to one another. This book will discuss eight. Some of them best convey comfort and consolation: listening, touching, giving, showing hospitality, helping, and praying. Those of speaking and writing can console and can "exhort" or prod to action.

We need both aspects of encouragement "as the day approaches." God doesn't want us to stay parked under broom trees.

PART II

The Methods of Encouragement

Warming Up Winter 3

*One kind word can warm up three winter
months.* —Japanese proverb

A lonely apartment on a frigid Chicago night can be an excellent stage for the gloomies to strut upon. That's how tonight started. Only a wall away, the wind whipped around yesterday's snowfall, driving temperatures to a *minus* forty-five-degree chill factor. Even long underwear and a thick afghan didn't help as I settled down to edit chapter 2. Besides, my mind kept going to an icy remark somebody had made that day.

Just as my rocker started warming up, the telephone rang. *Probably a wrong number,* I muttered as I flung aside my cold-night wrappings. I'd been getting plenty of false calls since the local college accidentally listed my phone number for one of its most popular coeds.

"Keeping warm?" the voice asked. Quickly I realized this voice was twenty-four hundred miles away—a neighbor back in my old hometown. Hearing a news report about Chicago's cold, she called to see how I was doing.

I was cheered and encouraged—and warmed up for the rest of the night!

There is truth to that Japanese saying, "One kind word can warm three winter nights." Even Mark Twain, not known to be a very vain man, once confessed that he could live three weeks on a compliment. Proverbs 12:25 says, "Anxiety in the heart of a man weighs it down, but a good word makes it glad."

Ministers of discouragement

When we speak to one another to affirm, comfort, or otherwise show we care, we can become ministers of encouragement. But speaking can also be a dangerous thing. Proverbs 18:21 says, "Death and life are in the power of the tongue." The apostle James warned, "From the same mouth come both blessing and cursing" (James 3:10).

A fellow named David knew all about that. The shrimp of his family, he had seven elder brothers built like trucks with macho prairie-tans to boot. When his brothers went off to war, David had to stay home with the family sheep. But David didn't mind. Contemplative and creative, he used quiet days in the pastures to write hymns and pray.

After a while his dad Jesse got concerned for the sons at the war front. Tucking a care package of cheese sandwiches under David's arm, he sent him off to bring back word of the war. David found his brothers and other soldiers waiting for the cold war to explode into something big. They were tense, anxious. Were they happy to see David and munch on goodies from home? Guess again.

"Some help you are," the oldest brother scoffed. "I suppose you told the lambies to take care of themselves while you cavorted around the countryside looking for entertainment and excitement!"

Or as 1 Samuel 17:28 recounts:

> Why have you come down? And with whom have you left those few sheep in the wilderness? I know your insolence and the wickedness of your heart; for you have come down in order to see the battle.

David's brother accused him of being a neglectful shepherd and coming out for fun—when instead the junior shepherd was only obeying orders from home. If I'd been David, I might have scuttled home crying.

But we know the rest of the story well. Over by the royal tent was somebody who would make up for the guff David got from his brothers. King Saul's son Jonathan watched David stomp toward the enemy's line of offensive (named Goliath), scoop some stones out of the creek, declare his defense of God's honor, and swing his sling hard. The earth jumped in shock as the giant collapsed, dead.

The rock-slinger who had endured his brothers' mud-slinging became a national hero. And he gained for a friend a prince who stuck by him from then on—who became his encourager. Later Jonathan's kind words warmed not just three winter months but the several years that David was a fugitive from Saul's death campaign.

We all need friends whose "pleasant words are a honeycomb, sweet to the soul and healing to the bones" (Prov. 16:24). Often those people seem to be bottled sunshine.

"One lady in our church always has a big smile on her face," one pastor told me. "She can say, 'You're so wonderful,' and you really do feel wonderful. She knows how to encourage people with compliments that come out of her heart. There's nothing phony about her. It's just a pattern of her life. And it's sure great to have her around."

The caring encourager

Such people can "warm winters" in three ways. First, they can pull the discouraged out of their holes, showing them that somebody *does* care. That's what happened with my winter night telephone call. The warmth of my friend's concern and interest melted away the gloom.

The Lord Jesus yearns to do this for us. When I'm discouraged I'm often drawn back to Psalm 40.

I waited patiently for the LORD;

And He inclined to me, and heard my cry.
He brought me up out of the pit of destruction, out of
   the miry clay;
And He set my feet upon a rock making my footsteps
   firm.
And He put a new song in my mouth, a song of praise
   to our God (Psalm 40:1-3).

"Pit" and "miry clay" describe discouragement so well. We
feel helpless, unable to rise, our feet trapped in a goo we
can't escape alone. Sometimes others may not realize how
much a good word can be a rope to pull us up.

The Rev. Leroy "Pat" Patterson, chaplain at Wheaton
College, once held a chapel service for a professional
baseball team. Noticing one player seemed especially
discouraged, he told him, "My daughter-in-law is a real
baseball fan and she's been a fan of yours for years. She'd be
really interested to know that I've talked to you."

The surprised player remarked, "You don't know what
that means. I decided just this morning that I was going to
quit baseball."

Praising the player's ability, Patterson encouraged him to
stay in pro ball and promised to pray for him. The next week
the player wrote Patterson that he'd decided to stay on. That
word of encouragement was what he needed.

Patterson remembers how something similar happened
years before during his student days at Wheaton. Financial
troubles and the press of studies had brought on discouragement. One day a professor stopped him as he walked out of
a history lecture.

"I've been watching you and you look really down," the
professor said. "I'm wondering what's the matter. Don't
forget, you're not here by accident. God led you here and
He will see you through."

The remark, Patterson says, "came when I needed it
most."

Speaking Scripture

Often, sharing Scriptures can be a way to speak encouragement. The summer I finished my graduate program I frequently saw another student who, like me, was finding job possibilities thinned by the national recession. As the weeks crept by, we both wondered why God had delayed answering our prayers for jobs.

But this friend faithfully looked for encouragement in God's Word and wasn't above looking in it for others.

"I've found just the Scripture for you," she phoned me one day. "Hebrews 6:10: 'For God is not unjust so as to forget your work and the love which you have shown toward His name, in having ministered and in still ministering to the saints.' Jeanne, you've been faithful to the Lord. He will be faithful to you. I just know it!"

I wrote that verse out on a three-by-five card and put it above my desk. Eventually we both found jobs, but in the meantime her warm words helped me.

The affirming encourager

Spoken words can "warm a winter" a second way when they affirm a person and help him build up positive qualities. Especially should verbal affirmation characterize Christian homes. Not only mates, but children need to hear they are important and cherished.

One Christmas time, for example, my five-year-old nephew David-John secretly glued four rocks on a plank from his father's firewood pile. Then he drew faces on the rocks to represent his family. He slid the creation under his sister's bed for safekeeping until Christmas Eve.

At gift-opening time he proudly brought it out. His mother hugged him, his father inspected it with positive remarks, and even his seven-year-old sister admitted, "That's pretty good, David-John."

When holiday visitors came, his mother made sure they saw David-John's project. "And he did it all by himself," she boasted loudly, so that he could hear. Next to the smallest in his kindergarten class, almost overshadowed by a can-do-everything sister, that affirmation was sunshine to his soul.

"In many little ways," Dorothy Briggs writes in *Your Child's Self-Esteem*, "we forget to focus on the unique gifts of each child. We focus on what he doesn't have. When we habitually attend to what's missing, cherishing gets lost. If your child lacks faith in himself, search to find what he can do. Give him plenty of recognition for those things and refuse to focus on what he cannot do. His sense of success—victory—is the key to his belief in himself. It feeds his conviction that he has something to offer, which spurs him on to new efforts."[5]

I started violin in a school orchestra program in seventh grade, surrounded by peers who'd been playing since fourth grade. Although I knew how to read music, I was frustrated because all my fingers felt like thumbs and my bow duplicated the screech of a braking locomotive. As I tearfully practiced at home, our family's two Siamese cats wandered around the house yowling their protest. Buried in the balcony of the second violin section, I labeled myself "hopeless."

One day the orchestra director took me aside to check my progress. As I grew red-faced and blinked back tears, he waited gently and then said kindly, "I know you want to play well, and I want you to know you're doing just great. You've really improved fast. Just keep in there. I'm proud of you."

That affirmation gave me the incentive to keep going. Five years later I sat as concertmistress—first chair—of the high school orchestra. If I'd listened to peers (or the family cats), I wouldn't have made it. But somebody who saw my struggle and encouraged me verbally made the difference.

Children, of course, thrive on competition and find it hard to say kind things about each other. But one of my former pastors, Kent Hughes, says it is sometimes his family's practice at dinner to single out one member for special affirmation.

"All of us have to tell at least one good thing we like about that person," he says. "An hour before dinner the kids may have been fighting with each other, but when dinner comes they know they'll have to say something positive. They'll have to admit, 'He's neat,' or 'She's kind.' "

Both he and his wife encourage their children for academic performance or other types of achievement, but Hughes says he gives double encouragement for displays of positive character, especially in their relationships with others. It may be a simple word such as, "I saw what you did for your sister and I appreciated that. It really showed character."

Our work relationships are another way to encourage the struggling. John Alexander of Inter-Varsity Christian Fellowship sees encouragement as one of an executive's most important personnel tools.

"Those whom we lead are soldiers in vigorous warfare," he says. "At times they will need balm on their wounds and rest from the fray. When discouragement shatters their spirits, may we be ready with some words of encouragement to lift their sagging souls."

He told of one secretary who had typed her way through a dictation belt her boss mailed in from his business trip. At the end she heard, "Thanks very much for doing these letters, Mary. I don't know how I'd get along without you, even though I don't say it very often."

The secretary's response? "I've been typing faster for three weeks on the strength of that word of praise!"[6]

Verbal encouragement also aids in the healing of grieving

persons. As part of their grief, they may think back over ways they failed the person who died. They may try to assume responsibility for the death. Their guilt and depression may make them ask whether life is worth living. But the encourager can defuse those negative feelings by looking for opportunities to affirm. Listening, touching, and writing (discussed in other chapters) are important, but the immediate feedback of verbal encouragement can heal the pain of the moment.

After my father's death, my grief-prompted discouragement was compounded by physically exhausting cleanup and mentally confusing probate. But one neighbor always had a compliment when she called or stopped by. She'd remark about how neatly I'd arranged a garage sale, or how nice the yard looked, or how quickly I had finished painting a room, or how conscientiously I was handling the probate paperwork. I needed to hear that—to know that I had value and that God still had purpose for me beyond the tasks that death had thrown in my lap.

Verbal encouragement can also be a means of showing the love of Christ to nonbelievers. Ed Coray, for many years a coach at Wheaton College, remembers one student named Archie who set the example of encouraging others with a good word. Whenever the team stopped to eat, Archie sought out the restaurant's proprietor to thank him for the service the roomful of young men had received.

"Lots of times, when people gave us service, Archie would go out of his way to thank them," Coray says. "He knew that a few thoughtful words can mean a lot to a person."

And the proprietor would link up that courtesy, of course, with the impression of a Christian college.

The exhorting encourager

A third way words can encourage is through what many would not consider positive strokes: exhortation. But because the Greek word for encouragement, *paraklesis,* means "comfort" as well as "exhortation," we're still treading the same ground. I look at "exhortation" as dealing with potential or existing negatives in an attempt to turn them into positives.

The apostles' teaching often dealt with the possibility of negatives spoiling the new faith of converts. When they "exhorted" they urged people to walk aright. Paul, for example, exhorted people to "walk in a manner worthy of the calling with which you have been called" (Eph. 4:1).

That sort of spirit was behind a confrontation between one of my former teachers, James L. Johnson, and a friend. Johnson had quit writing after he became a Christian in 1951, believing that writing was not the way he could best serve the Lord. Instead, he tried the mission field and pastorate. One day while pastoring a church in Chicago, Johnson ran into Ken Taylor, then an editor at Moody Press.

"Why don't you get back to that typewriter and see what you can write?" Taylor said.

Johnson was stunned by the suggestion. Taylor (who would later become internationally known for the paraphrased *Living Bible*) was insistent. Johnson went to his typewriter and pounded out "Wings of Eagles," a story that was accepted by *Christian Life* magazine and published in three parts.

That story broke open a dam of writing that by 1980 resulted in twelve books and more than a hundred magazine articles. And it propelled Johnson into a fruitful teaching career.

Just as Barnabas saw untapped potential in Paul, Taylor saw a locked-up gift in Johnson.

But an exhorter isn't always popular. Few want to be told they're headed in the wrong direction. The spiritual surgeon needs patients who won't kick too much under the knife. Proverbs says, "A rebuke goes deeper into one who has understanding, than a hundred blows into a fool" (17:10).

Exhortation must be tempered with love. Paul told Timothy to preach, reprove, rebuke and exhort—but "with great patience and instruction" (2 Tim. 4:2). Love prevents exhortation from becoming a negative criticism that wounds without healing. In his booklet *Practical Criticism*, John Alexander suggests that those who must criticize others should make the criticism constructive by including remedial suggestions.

"Loveless negative criticism is a prime component of worldliness," he says. "It is also one of the burdens of leaders. The spirit of a Christless society is to gossip, ridicule, focus on mistakes, and emphasize weaknesses of leaders. Our nation is riddled with critics who can point out what's wrong with nary a word of how to make it better. Rare indeed is the individual who can temper the indictment with a commensurate dose of viable options."[7]

He said a positive criticism should have these three parts.

1. Here is what I think you should stop doing.
2. Here is what I think you should start doing.
3. Here is what I think you should continue doing, but I believe it would be better if you did it this way.

The encourager's heart

Whether it be consolation or exhortation, verbal encouragement must begin with the right motives. Jude, for example, saw plenty of people engage in flattery but he also saw through them. He called them "grumblers, finding fault, following after their own lusts; they speak arrogantly, flattering people for the sake of gaining an advantage" (Jude 16).

Jesus pointed out how problems with what we say originate in problems of the heart (Matt. 15:18). Paul had that in mind when he urged the Philippians to think on those things that were honorable, right, pure, lovely, of good repute, showing excellence, and worthy of praise (Phil. 4:8). The person who grumbles and dwells on negatives can rarely be a verbal encourager.

Paul dug into the problem even deeper when he suggested that a Christian's "mouthset" should be characterized by this.

> Let no unwholesome word proceed from your mouth, but only such a word as is good for edification according to the need of the moment, that it may give grace to those who hear (Eph. 4:29).

The word "unwholesome" literally means "putrid" or "rotten." Few of us enjoy being around someone with bad breath—much less a bad mouthset. Instead, according to that verse, what we say should be edifying, timely, and Christ-conveying.

I thought of those three ingredients one time when I passed a neighbor in the utility room of our apartments. She spoke to me of her sister, newly-widowed and visiting her for an extended time until her health improved. My neighbor started talking of how the sister's family neglected her. My mind raced. It wasn't my place to disparage the sister's family—I didn't know them. And I was not part of the problem. What could I say that would be edifying, timely, and Christ-conveying? Gently I said, "You are a very special person for this hard time of her life. I honor what you're doing."

We cannot speak encouragement to one another when hatred contaminates our hearts. Once I worked with another person who always spoke harshly and negatively to me. At one point she admitted she was jealous of me and even though we talked through the problem she still seemed to harbor bitterness. I was tempted to bite back, but instead prayed that God would fill me with love for her and make my speech encouraging to her. As He did, her attitude and speech mellowed. Paul urged the same.

> Let all bitterness and wrath and anger and clamor and slander be put away from you, along with all malice. And be kind to one another, tender-hearted, forgiving each other, just as God in Christ also has forgiven you (Eph. 4:31-32).

Knowing that God has forgiven me, not only for my sinful nature but also for the sins I commit with my tongue, gives me the courage to go on speaking to others. My pride is not threatened when I compliment them; my courage is not shredded if I seek to turn them to God's perspective.

I'll admit it sometimes takes nerve, which I don't have in abundance. But I am learning to be obedient to the Holy Spirit's promptings to verbally affirm other people. For me it helps to preface a remark with, "Can I be serious and tell you something I appreciate about you?" or "At the risk of embarrassing you, I'd like to tell you something very special."

One day I told a pastor, "You may think this sounds strange, but I just want to thank you for the way you sometimes preach through tears. It shows me you're a man who really cares." He bowed his eyes and said softly, "Thanks, I appreciate that."

My years in journalism have shown me how editors are not famous as encouragers. Give an editor a pencil and a manuscript and within minutes it will look like a strategy map—circles, arrows, cross-outs all over. Sometimes I've had my own manuscripts so thoroughly re-edited by someone else that I could barely recognize them (or read through the scribbles to retype them!). It's a vocation in which it's easy to become cynical.

In our Christian lives we will have times when we need to "edit" one another. But while we "edit" we must also be conscious of the positives and speak out encouragement.

Walter MacPeek said it well in his "Manuscript Reader's Prayer."

> Today I ask, O Father, that I may be an encourager,
> that I may find some glimmer of promise
> which I may encourage to grow;
> Grant me the strength to be generous
> in my words of commendation;
> Give me the perceptiveness and the insight
> to respond to thoughts that may touch the heart,
> as well as the mind. [8]

Booster Shots

I am sending him to you for just this purpose, to let you know how we are and be encouraged by his report. —The apostle Paul (Eph. 6:22 TLB)

One of the real nobodies of the New Testament is a fellow by the name of Tertius. We have only one verse about him at the tail end of Paul's masterpiece letter to the Romans. "I, Tertius, who write this letter, greet you in the Lord" (Rom. 16:22).

All we know is that he wrote the Roman letter at Paul's dictation in Corinth. He was a secretary—maybe a first century version of temporary help or maybe just a believer who felt his spiritual service could be his penmanship.

What arouses my curiosity, however, is why Tertius even bothered to write a P.S. Perhaps he knew the people in Rome. But I wonder if he simply cared enough for others in the body of Christ to write "howdy," even if it had to be a miniscule postscript. He wanted to remind others that he, too, was "in the Lord."

I like that sort of spirit.

We often think of "encouragement" as something we do by what we say. But some of my greatest encouragement has come through written means—when people cared enough to *write* what was on the surface on their hearts.

Written encouragement can pack more power than verbal for two reasons. First, we're less apt to be shy on paper. Paul admitted to that. "I . . . am meek when face to face with you, but bold toward you when absent" (2 Cor. 10:1). In person he may have come across like a soggy gym towel. But his pen packed dynamite.

Second, what is written can encourage over and over. When someone writes to encourage me, I reread that note so often I almost memorize it. The notes become self-administered booster shots or, as Proverbs puts it, "like cold water to a weary soul" (Prov. 25:25).

The Christian community is all the richer when people tap into this potent ministry. In Salem, Oregon, for example, the Christian and Missionary Alliance church plans as part of its worship service a time for members to write "encouragement" on cards kept in the pew racks.

Pastor Don Bubna started the practice after observing the use of prayer cards in another church. It occurred to him that members should not only register their prayer needs, but visually tell of their love and concern for one another.

Thus his Sunday service now includes a time after the sermon for people to pray for others in silence and then to jot a short message on the postcard-sized "encouragement cards," which are later collected in offering plates for the church to mail or deliver.

"Learning to be an encourager is a long process," Bubna says. "It means getting in the habit of thinking well of others and letting them know it. The cards are a tangible tool, something we can go back and look at, again and again, and it cheers us every time."

And people really appreciate the gesture. Bubna remembers visiting a dying church member in a nursing home. Too ill to speak, she gestured for her Bible and from it pulled a treasured encouragement card.

"It consisted of just seven words saying that she was remembered and appreciated," Bubna says, "but it brightened her life."[9]

The writing practice

The method of the Salem church seems to have broken through the excuses people use for not writing. Some claim, "I don't have time." But the worship service provides the time.

Others complain, "I don't have nice stationery." Post cards are plain and cheap—but the message they carry is priceless.

"My handwriting and grammar are too awful," has been another consideration. But there's not much room for error on a three-by-five inch piece of paper. If people crave encouragement, they'll wade through the externals and remember the heart of the message.

"Written encouragement" doesn't need to be limited to a church service, however. It can be a lifestyle, as it is for Ed Coray, a longtime coach and now senior alumni director at Wheaton College, Illinois.

"I like people, and I like to get in touch," he says. "A long time ago I read about the practice of writing at least three notes a day just to encourage people. Maybe these people are going through hard times such as a death or illness. Maybe they've achieved something or been promoted. I just write them about it."

Brief and sincere, his notes go out to professors, students, alumni, and parents. He also writes people too old to write back (one is more than one hundred years old) "because I want to remind them that someone hasn't forgotten them."

Once an alumni mother wrote him about her concern for her son, a professional athlete whom she felt had an aptitude for working with young people. Coray promised to pray (another aspect of encouragement) and then started watching papers for stories on the young man.

One time the sports section reported that he'd been benched by an injury. Later Coray spotted pictures of him playing with residents of a farm for retarded persons and visiting children's hospitals.

He sent her those clippings and wrote, "It looks like your prayers might soon be answered." For that mother and son, Coray was a link of information and encouragement.

The secrets of easier writing

When I was writing this chapter, someone said, "Hey, I'm no writer. I just can't put words on paper. Besides, I barely have time to write home to the folks. Forget the encouragement note business."

It's true that some people seem to have clogged passages between their minds and pens. But I'll tell you a secret: those passages tend to unclog with use. The more you write, the easier it gets.

And it isn't a secret that we find time for what we want to do. If people matter, then look procrastination in the eye and *do it*. If you type easily, type the notes—and forget any rumor about typed notes being "improper."

Make writing convenient for you. One person I know keeps a supply of post cards in her Bible. Sometimes during her devotional times she recalls someone she wants to encourage—and then writes something brief. Another puts notepaper in her car's glove compartment or purse. When she has a spare moment—while waiting in the car or for a meeting to start—she jots a message to somebody whom God has put on her heart.

Take some hints from the pros. When you visit a card shop, spend some time reading the unrhymed messages. Don't plagiarize, but adapt the ones that sound like you. If words still come hard, try a rough draft on any old scrap of paper. And, if you're uneasy about your grammar, ask someone close to read over your draft.

If you truly want to encourage, the Lord will supply the

right words and make them communicate. And He also will point out to you those who need the boost of written encouragement.

Who needs it?

Often they are the sick. Bubna says when his congregation zeroes in on those who are ill or in the hospital, "it's a great joy to take them a stack of cards too thick to put in one envelope. Just imagine the lift it gives to be the recipient of so much compassion."[10]

When, as a child, I was bed-bound with rheumatic fever, the daily deluge of get-well cards not only cheered me but encouraged my parents. Those cards told them somebody cared about the hard time they were going through.

Twenty years later, another set of cards cheered me when I was bed-bound with a terrific case of the Mexican missionary miseries (amoebic dysentery), which plunged my weight to a bony eighty-five pounds. When a co-worker delivered a stack of cards—many of them homemade—I realized how much people missed me and loved me.

One of the directors' wives had taken a minute to add this note to her card. "As I was reading in Isaiah this morning I wanted to claim this verse for you as we all pray for your recovery. Read Isaiah 58:11 but don't read it in the King James!" Of course, I disobeyed, and smiled when I read, "And the Lord shall guide thee continually . . . *and make fat thy bones.*"

Scriptures telling of comfort and hope are also appropriate to share with those who are terminally ill. As they struggle through accepting their approaching deaths, they need to know that they are loved and their lives have been worthwhile. They need to know people are praying. A few written words—telling of your care and of things you appreciate about them—can pack sunshine.

One pastor encouraged a little girl dying of cancer by writing letters on big paper bags that supposedly were from his horse. The imaginary correspondence brightened her last painful weeks.

Sympathy cards can encourage the bereaved even more when they contain a few words of personal encouragement. When my own parents died, I wept throught the stacks of sympathy cards that came. But I was encouraged when people took the time to write something special that they remembered about Mom or Dad. Since then I've been challenged to make my "sympathy notes" more than rote phrases by adding something positive to help the bereaved.

When a friend buried his father, I was moved to write, "Although I never knew your father, I can't help but believe that the sensitivity to people that characterizes your life was also true of his. Your daily care for others' needs is the greatest legacy you can carry on from him."

I've learned, too, that sympathy notes needn't be limited to the time right after a death. Four years after a Chrisitan couple lost a teen-age son, someone wrote them a four-page, single-spaced letter recalling that son's spiritual ministry. The letter greatly encouraged and comforted them.

Those who are lonely, weak in faith, or low in self-esteem can especially be helped by spontaneous written encouragement. I've sometimes found that little notes I felt prompted to send reached somebody just when they were going through a tough time and needed to know that somebody cared.

I've experienced that in my own life, too. When I entered short-term mission service, I faced many scary unknowns, including a move to a strange city and an unpredictable support allowance. But my wobbly faith was steadied as I started to receive notes, cards, and financial gifts from a couple I'd met only once during my deputation. When they took the time to write, I knew they were thinking of me. And when they said they were praying for me, I believed it.

Even after I completed my mission service, they didn't forget me. They continued to write and even sent money to help with Bible school expenses. Later, they wrote whenever they noticed one of my articles had been published. At just the right times, I was boosted.

Their love, expressed through regular contact, convicted me of an area of writing where I had failed: corresponding with missionaries I supported financially or in prayer.

Missionaries I've talked to say that mail call is the most exciting part of their day (or week or month, when they live in remote places). Even the apostle Paul, back when mail was barely a lick and a promise, looked forward to correspondence from his "mission fields" and supporters. The New Testament contains some of those letters of encouragement and challenge that he sent to young churches and aspiring pastors.

At times Paul sent his letters with a flesh-and-blood return envelope. "I hope in the Lord Jesus to send Timothy to you shortly, so that I also may be encouraged when I learn of your condition" (Phil. 2:19).

A "here's what's happening" letter

I like that phrase "your condition." It can include the meat-and-potatoes part of living as well as the spiritual. Missionaries are human; letters to them don't have to sound like theological treatises.

During my time as a short-term missionary (in the "jungles" of Los Angeles) I appreciated letters that included a humorous incident or some child's newest joke. (Humor is the missionary's relief valve.) I enjoyed it when friends tucked in photos, clippings from the hometown newspaper, or personal notes from children, which I proudly posted in my office area.

I appreciated those who asked about progress in an area I'd asked prayer for. And I wanted to share their prayer needs. I was edified when they told me what God had been teaching them, since often I was facing struggles calling for the same spiritual principles.

Take, for example, this letter.

> An older brother, who has known the Lord for forty-four years, who writes this, says for your encouragement that He has never failed him. In the greatest difficulties, in the heaviest trials, in the deepest poverty and necessities, He has never failed me; but because I was enabled by His grace to trust in Him, He has always appeared for my help. I delight speaking well of His name.[11]

That didn't come to me but was written a century ago to Hudson Taylor, missionary to China. The author: George Muller, man of faith, founder of orphanages in Bristol, England—a "home" missionary himself. What a boost that letter must have been!

Over the last few years I've discovered the fragrance of writing "encouragement" to those who've helped me. I became sensitive in this area after taking to heart the lesson of the ten lepers that Jesus healed on His way through Samaria. Only one returned to thank the Savior for his healing, and he was a Samaritan. Jesus asked (and, I imagine, with sadness in His voice) "Were there not ten cleansed? But the nine—where are they? Were none found who turned back to give glory to God, except this foreigner?" (Luke 17:17-18).

I've tried to write teachers and professors, former bosses, former colleagues—and there are probably more I should write.

A few years ago, for example, gratitude welled up in my heart for the pastor whose preaching nudged me toward surrendering my life to Jesus Christ. He probably never knew it—I was just one of those collegians who filled up his pews every Sunday and dropped a pittance in the plate. But his humility and great love for Jesus had communicated to me.

By chance I learned that he had transferred to another church. Halfway apologizing, I wrote him, thanking him for his faithfulness in reaching out to the college crowd, and telling him what it had meant to my life. I don't know how he reacted to that letter but later, when I visited his new church and introduced myself, he was so full of joy that his handshake nearly dislocated my shoulder.

I know of others who have discovered the sweetness of affirming their families and close friends through written words. One man's personal treasures include a shoe box full of love messages his wife wrote on napkins she packed in his lunch. He couldn't bear to toss them out with the banana peels.

Another husband sends his wife love cards from the office. One close family puts notes to each other throughout the house. The mother found a love note taped to the milk in the refrigerator one morning. The father found one taped to his steering wheel saying: "Daddy, I'm praying for the man who's a problem at work." He drove to work infused with hope.

I've noticed that families that drift apart are often ones that let communication slide when members leave home. It seems that out-of-sight means out-of-mind. One remedy could be a simple post card, which takes five minutes to fill and costs much less than a long-distance telephone call. Despite what a card says in print, it says silently: "Hey, you're missed. You're important to us. We love you." It girds up the family support system.

Some people use birthdays or anniversaries as special occasions to write encouraging notes. Instead of a commercial card, they send a letter of love. One young man, on his first wedding anniversary, thanked his in-laws by letter for preparing their daughter to be his wife. He told of her traits and skills that he appreciated. I'm sure his stock in that family went up several points.

Learning early

Writing encouragement is something parents can teach their children and turn into a family ministry. Most children enjoy coloring and creating. They also like to give their work away. I've wondered why more families don't establish "greeting card factories" and allow children to make original cards for birthdays, anniversaries, or illnesses.

Not only would they save money, but the message would be personalized. And the children would derive great pleasure from knowing their work had a purpose and a destination. The recipients wouldn't be the only ones encouraged.

Because their parents' home and business were just a few doors away from a small-town newspaper office, my niece and nephew frequently had their pictures taken and published. A hot-day photo showed them playing in their little pool; another scorcher, at their own lemonade stand. After the big snow, David made the front page shoveling the sidewalk with a shovel almost as big as he.

One time as Christine walked home from school, a reporter called out and asked her to pose with the spring's first pussy willows. When I visited them the next weekend, I suggested that Christine write the reporter a thank-you for. choosing her for the picture, and for sending over afterwards the glossy print for the family scrapbook. While I sat at the sewing machine doing mending, Christine collapsed on the rug beside me with her stationery pad, colored felt-tip pens, and a puzzled look.

"What can I write?" she asked. I suggested a beginning

sentence and with that she set to work, slowly forming each letter to show off her best printing. At the bottom she drew a flower. Except for a little coaching on spelling, the work was her own.

A few days later the reporter's column included Christine's letter and a short postscript saying what a boost the little girl's note had been.

A letter timed rightly

One day at the card shop I noticed a "why-I-haven't-written" card. It said something to the effect that the sender had thought about writing three times, so the receiver now owed him three letters. I laughed, then put the card back sadly, thinking how one of the greatest tragedies of encouragement is the letter not sent and, along with that, the blessing when a letter came at exactly the right time.

A missionary friend, Helen, was packing up the family's rural house in Guatemala for their return to the city when she got a letter with bad news. A woman who had been a prayer supporter was seriously ill and not expected to live.

"Boxes were all over and I had much to do," Helen recalls, "but I felt I had to write her. I wanted to tell her how much I loved her and appreciated her life."

The next day the family made the wearying, twelve-hour drive to the city.

"When we arrived I asked my husband if we could mail the letter right away and if, instead of taking it to the post office, we could take it to the airport," she says.

As he let her off by the airport, Helen felt an urge to take the letter directly to a flight counter instead of putting it down the mail slot. The attendant told her it would go on the next flight. When the letter arrived in Oklahoma, a pastor's wife checked the woman's mailbox and immediately took the letter to the hospital.

"The pastor's wife later told me my friend was so far gone that she couldn't respond verbally," Helen says, "but as the pastor's wife read my letter, my dying friend squeezed her hand. Right afterwards, she slipped into her final coma. It meant so much to me that she had heard in time."

I could tell a similar story. My mother died just three months before my parents' thirty-eighth wedding anniversary. As the anniversary date (September 29) approached, I was halfway accross the country at graduate school, hurting deeply with Dad and wanting to assure him of my love on that lonely date.

I wrote neighbors and asked them to have him over for dinner that day. But I also knew within me that I had to write a special letter, something in addition to the weekly news notes I always wrote home.

I found a card that said, "When you are alone, Jesus is there." In that card, as tears streamed down my face, I wrote a letter of love, telling my dad things I'd never had the courage to say in person. I affirmed him for the way he took care of our family and especially Mom during the years of her illness.

I mailed it so it would arrive on the anniversary day. I learned later that he cried when he got the letter. And he shared it with a few close friends. Ten weeks later he died of a heart attack.

As I dropped out of school and flew home to settle affairs, I thought of the anniversary letter while I dumped out drawers and sorted through piles of mail. Had he kept it? Daddy usually saved everything of sentimental value. Or had the letter upset him so much that he destroyed it?

January passed, then February, as slowly I sorted out his and Mother's personal belongings. I found old birthday cards, my grade school papers, and letters ten and fifteen years old. But not *that* letter. Then in March I got to the closet where luggage was stored. In the pocket of the suit-

case he used on a trip the week before his death, there it
was.

He had kept it with him!

I opened it and cried again, thankful I'd written when
I did.

"Dear Daddy, I know this will be a very lonely
September 29 for you without Mom. I wish I could be
there to comfort you. I greatly miss her, too, and as I
write this the tears are coming so fast I have to blot my
face every few words. I don't know what it's like to cel-
ebrate an anniversary with one you love. Though I
would desire to be married, God has not granted that
privilege. But He did grant it to you and Mom, and
along with it He sent the sorrows and joys that
stretched you, refined you, and perfected you.

"I wasn't there, only a plan in God's mind, when
Mom's health necessitated the move to California in
the early 1940s. But I look back on that move as one illustration of a man who—despite the fragile uncertainties of the future—honored his commitment to love
and care for his wife. That takes a special man.

"The Lord, knowing Mom's needs, was infinitely
wise when He brought you together, and assigned
Mom's care to you (and your care, likewise, to her).
And that is hardly the beginning of the story because,
as He filled your quiver with two arrows (named Judith
and Jeanne), He deemed you worthy of caring for
them, too.

"I can't help but believe that the Lord has more tasks
for you as you have now greater resources in abilities
and time than ever before. And He will show you what
those tasks are to be.

"But while we wait—either for the hope of His calling or (maranatha!) the hope of His *coming*—we can
wait confidently that neither death nor life . . . things

present nor things to come . . . anything, in fact, nothing, 'shall be able to separate us from the love of God, which is in Christ Jesus, our Lord' (Rom. 8:39).

"I love you in a deep way . . . and God loves you *infinitely. Jeanne.*"

Each sentence had been hard to put down. I had hidden those dimensions of my gratitude too long.

Daddy's aloneness now is over. But I thank God that He prompted me to send that note of love and encouragement—in time.

The Silent Love 5

Anyone who thinks that his time is too valuable to spend keeping quiet will eventually have no time for God and his brother, but only for himself and his own follies. —Dietrich Bonhoeffer[12]

I considered introducing this chapter with an Old West version of a famous story of listening.

I could have told about Joe, a wealthy farmer with a brood of ten, respected in the community, faithful to fill a pew at church. The prairies had been good to him. His horses and cattle peacefully munched the greens. His ranch house viewed a craggy range above an endless meadow of daisies.

Then one day everything that could have gone wrong, went wrong. Some outlaws attacked and rustled his herd, killing all but one of his hands. On their hasty exit they set a prairie fire that roared over most of his holdings. His sons and daughters raced out of the house, grabbed their own horses and attempted to drive his flocks to the safety of a lake. Joe stayed home to wet down the roofs of his house and barns.

But the fire was fierce and a freak wind drove it right over the land, trapping his children and finally scorching the farm buildings. In a matter of hours Joe's world was reduced to embers. His wife, in town shopping when it all happened, returned to find him burned and dazed. He was rushed to the village clinic where the doctor only shook his head over Joe's condition. "So this is the sort of thing God does," Joe's wife scoffed as she left to stay at a friend's house.

As Joe's pain, loneliness, and agony crushed in on him, word spread fast to three old friends. Hurriedly they dropped their work and came to town. They could see he was hurting badly. There weren't words to express their concern. They just sat in silence for an entire week.

That might be a more modern rendering of the book of Job. But the prairie version doesn't begin to express the pathos that throbs through the Old Testament book. Like Joe, Job lost much. Everything, in fact, except a crabby wife. Sabeans took his oxen and donkeys. A fire destroyed his sheep. Chaldeans stole his camels. Each time, too, all but one servant perished. Then a tornado sucked up his sons and daughters. Finally he lost his health and sat in the town dump with painful, putrid, ulcerating sores. Nobody wanted to be near him. Even his wife (not known for her encouragement) complained, "You have rotten breath" (Job 19:17).

But three friends—Eliphaz, Bildad, and Zophar—cared enough to come and mourn wordlessly.

> They made an appointment together to come to sympathize with him and comfort him. And when they lifted up their eyes at a distance, and did not recognize him, they raised their voices and wept. And each of them tore his robe, and they threw dust over their heads toward the sky. Then they sat down on the ground with him for seven days and seven nights with no one speaking a word to him, for they saw that his pain was very great (Job 2:11-13).

In Oriental culture, sitting in silence, throwing dust, and tearing clothes was a way to express extraordinary grief (check Gen. 50:10, Josh. 7:6, 1 Sam. 31:13, Lam. 2:10, and Acts 22:23). But looking beyond the culture of grief, there is a great, deep hurt in the book of Job. To be around such a man today would strike us wordless.

Compassionate listening

After a week of silence, Job found the courage to say something. He told his friends he wished he'd never been born (chapter 3). How did his comforters respond? By becoming accusers. They added to his misery by preaching, by telling him God was punishing him for some sin, by tearing apart whatever courage he might have had. In the middle of their preaching Job finally cried out in frustration:

You are all worthless physicians.
O that you would be completely silent,
And that it would become your wisdom!
(Job 13:4b-5).

And later:

How long will you torment me,
And crush me with words? (19:2).

Job's reaction—until the voice of God thundered down to the ash heap—indicates he still needed compassionate listeners. Only later could he handle advice.

It's not much different today. We can encourage those who suffer greatly by offering our presence and our hearts. When people are stunned by a tragedy, they don't want someone clawing at their wounds. They want someone to come alongside and *be there.*

"Secular education today," wrote Dietrich Bonhoeffer, "is aware that often a person can be helped merely by having someone who will listen to him seriously, and upon this insight it has constructed its own soul therapy, which has attracted great numbers of people, including Christians. But Christians have forgotten that the ministry of listening has been committed to them by Him who is Himself the great listener and whose work they should share. We should listen with the ears of God that we may speak the Word of God."[13]

This means offering our *presence* as well as our *ears and hearts.* Our *presence* means we are willing to come. Our *ears and hearts* means we will offer our uncondemning attention.

When I think of "presence" I often am reminded of the story told of a little girl who went to comfort the mother of a playmate who recently died. When she came back, her own mother asked her what she had done to comfort the other mother. The little girl replied, "I just climbed up on her lap and cried with her."

The support of silence

In their own way, the three wise men did the same. They didn't consider themselves too important to drop their work to come and comfort Job. By coming, they provided a support system. (His wife certainly wasn't offering one.) Job could have felt he belonged nowhere, but with interested, sympathetic and accepting friends he could feel that someone else wanted to be involved in his hurt.

Especially is presence meaningful to the sick and grieving. Pain can wither their emotions and make them feel lonely. If that loneliness goes unchecked, they may think nobody cares about them and decide life isn't worth living. Going to a sick bed, holding a person's hand, sometimes just sitting wordlessly, helps them know they're not alone.

When grief from death is freshest, the words should be the fewest. The Joe Baylys lost three sons and he recalls, after the death of one, "I was sitting, torn by grief. Someone came and talked to me of God's dealings, of why it happened, of hope beyond the grave. He talked constantly, he said things I knew were true. I was unmoved, except to wish he'd go away. He finally did. Another came and sat beside me. He just sat beside me for an hour and more, listened when I said something, answered briefly, prayed simply, left. I was moved. I was comforted. I hated to see him go."[14]

Writer Keith Miller remembers something similar at his father's funeral. After the service, many came to the Miller home, including one tall man Miller remembers as having leathery skin and white hair. He sat all evening at one end of the couch holding his Stetson hat. Finally, when everyone else had gone, he came over to Miller. "Son," he said, "I knew your daddy and he was a fine man." He looked straight at Miller, shook hands, turned around and left.

"I have never forgotten that man, and I can't remember anyone else who came to call that night," Miller says. "The fact that he came and sat with us in our grief all evening, without having to say a thing, then finally made a comment about my dad and left was enough. That man had come for my father and for us. I can't even remember his name, but his presence had an enormous effect on me."

Since then, Miller has made an effort to attend funerals when loved ones of friends die. "I realize now," he says, "that most of the time it doesn't matter much what I say, if I can only be present. I think this is a basic truth about visiting people who are sick and perhaps even those in prison: it is not so important that you come with an articulate and convincing message as that you come and care."[15]

One day during the cleanup after my parents' deaths, I came on a task that proved too much for me alone. I had found several boxfuls of old family photos that I realized should be pasted in an album for my sister's safekeeping. But as I started the job in the silence of that house of memories, the job tore me apart. I crumbled in uselessness when I saw photos of my parents, younger and healthy.

In tears I went over to the neighbor, Carol. I knew I had to finish the job—and no one else could. She dropped her work, poured herself a cup of coffee, came over and sat on the floor near me while I finished pasting. She said little. But that hour or hour-and-a-half she just stayed with me comforted and encouraged.

A listening post ministry

But "silent love" requires more than being there. Paul Tournier, considered one of the great people-helpers of this century, was asked one time to share his secret for counseling. He replied, "I don't know how to help people. I simply listen and love and try to provide a safe place where people can come and report on their progress without any judgment."[16]

Listening means offering our uncondemning attention so a person can talk out his confused feelings. It helps if we realize that a person going through a traumatic situation is also going through a grief process.

Grief is not limited to death. Grief occurs when a significant person or object is cut out of a person's emotional constellation and he experiences pain. A person can grieve over a jilted romance, a pregnancy out of wedlock or an abortion, the birth of a handicapped child, a job loss, a business failure, or a shattered dream.

Grief is a complex emotion. It unknots slowly, only after much time and much talking out. Some people are so grateful for a listener that they don't need much prompting to talk. News services once told of a man who offered to listen to anyone by phone for $6 an hour. He was swamped with requests.

Others may need a listener who can help draw out their feelings. A listener might trigger talking by saying, "You must feel bewildered," "You're really hurting today, aren't you?", or, "I wish I could crawl inside you and bear your pain for a while for you."

A non-threatening setting can also help a person talk. Some may feel comfortable in a room, sitting across from another. Others may open up if they go on a walk or a ride. My dad's doctor had recommended that he walk to help his heart. After my mother's death I joined him a few times on those walks. As I listened I began to see a side of him that I'd never seen before, as this normally very private man opened up and shared his feelings.

Grieving step-by-step

Knowing the emotional journey that grief involves can help us be better listeners. A few years ago Elisabeth Kübler-Ross gained international attention with her research about the grief emotions of the terminally ill. But the list she proposed also describes other grieving processes, including deaths of hopes or dreams.

The first reaction is normally denial. The person rejects the trauma. He goes into shock attempting to say it didn't happen, yet realizing it has.

Next, he expresses anger. He blames others for what has happened.

Third, he often experiences guilt by turning his anger inward. He blames himself for what happened.

Fourth, he experiences genuine grief, and goes through depression and crying spells.

Fifth, he is able to accept the crisis and go on to reconstruct his life.

In all these stages, the presence of a listener is important although his role diminishes. Right after a death, for example, people want other people around so they don't feel alone. The same for those going through a divorce. But, like Job, they don't want sermons. They want silence, listeners.

When the hurting person wants to talk about the crisis—or his anger or his guilt—the listener should not try to change the subject. The details may be retold several times, the same ideas expressed, but in the process he will move toward healing.

Some hurts don't heal easily. Divorce, for example, is difficult in Christian circles when other believers treat the divorcing as social lepers. Death is easier to accept, because it has a finality and neither party is normally to blame. But those who listen, offering acceptance and support, will help a person go a long way toward reconstructing a life.

Listening requires loving patience; healing may take months or sometimes years. I remember how several didn't forget me and my need for listeners after my parents' deaths. One widow who had never known me—only my parents—called at least once a week for several months. Her first question was, "I just wondered how you are doing?" She was an uncondemning, comforting listener.

Others invited me to their homes for dinner. After spending days alone cleaning and sorting through belongings, I nearly burst with the need to talk. And the more I talked, the less the conversations were about "me" and "death" and more about "you" and "us." Healing came.

Some also thoughtfully realized that certain occasions—holidays, or anniversaries of births or deaths—were hard for me to handle alone. An elderly friend I call "Grandma" jolted me out of bed with a sunrise phone call on December 12—exactly one year after my father's death. By that time I was back in graduate school but the date was still a sad reminder.

"I know what this day is for you," she said in a familiar, comforting vioce. "I just wanted to tell you that I love you." Someone who had buried her parents and husband knew my weakness—and cared. As we talked I could recount God's faithfulness over the past years, and one more victory marked my journey back from grief.

We shouldn't think, however, that quality listening is a ministry we should limit to those going through major traumatic incidents. Sometimes it's not just one big volcanic event that crushes somebody but a series of cactus-size thorns that pain him to the edge of endurance. I think that's often what the apostle Paul experienced—and why he in one epistle expressed gratefulness for a listener.

During one of his trips through Macedonia, he'd gone through the works. "Our flesh had no rest," he wrote the Corinthians. "But we were afflicted on every side: conflicts without, fears within" (2 Cor. 7:5).

He was despaired, torn up. Yet the God whose eyes run to and fro throughout the whole earth showing Himself faithful to those who know Him (2 Chron. 16:9) had seen all this too.

"God, who comforts the depressed," Paul added, "comforted us by the coming of Titus." Titus was one of the young men Paul had discipled for the ministry. Here was a case of the junior encouraging and comforting the senior. The passage says Titus brought some good reports of the church to boost Paul's spirits. But I doubt if Titus did all the talking when the two got together. I imagine Titus was also a patient, loving listener.

There was no need for Titus to preach at Paul. Paul knew enough about suffering to write several books. But he hurt. He needed no jolly rendition of "I've got a joy, joy, joy, joy." (Prov. 25:20 warns, "Like one who takes off a garment on a cold day . . . is he who sings songs to a troubled heart"!) Instead there was quiet, caring listening.

The cost of listening

Sharing griefs and hurts by listening takes time, but being willing to provide that time is a mark of spiritual maturity. One man says he has learned to save up chunks and pieces of time to give away to people as tithes of himself. Thus when people interrupt him or need someone to talk to, his focus can go to their spiritual needs instead of to his deadlines.

Being willing to listen often results from once needing listeners ourselves. In his classic devotional, *My Utmost for*

His Highest, Oswald Chambers wrote: "If a man has not been through the fires of sorrow, he is apt to be contemptuous, he has no time for you. If you receive yourself in the fires of sorrow, God will make you nourishment for other people."[17]

Encouraging people in crises may come with a high cost. A friend from another country, studying in the U.S., decided to visit a church of her ethnic background. In the church's rest room she met a woman who had recently been through a divorce and lacked the support of a listener. The divorcée was so desperate to be loved and affirmed that she spilled out her story of sorrow right there to a stranger.

As a result of that encounter, my friend decided to spend time with the woman until she completed her studies. This meant taking a long train ride, losing weekend study time, and forfeiting much of her own privacy. But she was willing to pay that cost.

The more we know God, the more we realize His great love in listening to us at any time, any place, and for any reason. "I love the Lord," the Psalmist said, "because He hears my voice and my supplications" (Psalm 116:1). And our love for God is expressed in our love for others. Bonhoeffer observed, "Just as love to God begins with listening to His word, so the beginning of love for the brethren is learning to listen to them."[18]

And that sometimes means being willing to be a listener when we'd rather be listened to.

When Helen, a friend, underwent gall bladder surgery, she didn't believe the doctor's prognosis that it would take six months of rest for her to recover. A missionary, mother of eight, and now graduate student in counseling psychology, Helen said: "I thought that would never be true of me. I had too much to do to sit around." But her body rebelled when she tried to resume her former schedule. She became depressed and frustrated.

"When people at church asked, 'How are you doing?' I wanted to tell them the truth—but I couldn't," Helen said. "The truth was that I didn't feel at all well. I started to get very defensive about it all."

At that time another woman in church, who had gone through two gall bladder surgeries in four months, started calling.

"She's a shy person and before that I had never gotten to know her," Helen says. "But she really understood. She would listen while I talked, and her message through all of it would be, 'I've been there. I know what it's like.' That gave me freedom to tell her honestly about my depression, my lack of energy, my defensiveness—about how I really felt."

As their friendship developed over the phone, the other woman started having symptoms of illness and learned she had Hodgkin's disease.

"Now the roles have been reversed," Helen says. "She calls about once a week and sometimes I'm on the phone with her an hour. We've had some in-depth conversations about death and the meaning of suffering. Because she provided a climate where I could level with her, now she can do the same with me."

Listening—the quiet love—costs. But that cost pays eternal dividends.

A Touch Kindly Spoken 6

My name is written on His hands. — Charles Wesley.

Tucked away in a corner of Isaiah is a verse that's easily missed—unless you have seen, as I have, an unforgettable illustration of it.

> Behold, I have inscribed you on the palms of
>   My hands;
> Your walls are continually before me.

I saw Isaiah 49:16 in a wood carving, finely-sanded and oiled, that showed a child hugging the palm of a giant hand. The artist had cut it to remember this verse.

Some scholars say the verse refers to an ancient Jewish custom of puncturing a representation of Jerusalem's walls and temple on the hands, as a reminder and symbol of their zeal for the holy city.

Through Isaiah, and this image, God is telling Israel that He will never forget His chosen people. His love will be even more faithful than mother love:

> Can a woman forget her nursing child
> And have no compassion on the son of her womb?
> Even these may forget, but I will not forget you (49:15).

Even a mother could forget the fruit of her womb. But God would never turn His back on Israel.

God chose the primary limb of touching—the hand—to convey an image of caring. We often think of communicating "I care" through what we write or say. But a touch kindly spoken can show caring like no other form of

72

communication. Social scientists, in fact, say that only a fourth of human communication is verbal. More than we realize is relayed nonverbally—by body actions, facial expressions, and other aspects of our culture such as smell and sound.

Yet touch can be a beautiful tool of encouragement.

The touch of His hand

Some of the gospels' most poignant passages show Jesus touching people. Even though His culture had taboos about touching "unclean" things, there was a freedom to reach out and make contact, to let people know that He wanted to minister to them.

And when I see Him extending His hands to people, I see the perfect High Priest offering up sacrifices of love acceptable to the Father.

One time I read the gospel of Mark just to notice His touching. He took Peter's sick mother-in-law by the hand and helped her up, healing her (Mark 1:31). Then He touched a leper (1:41). People pushed forward to touch Him, hoping for healing (3:10). Jairus, the synagogue ruler, begged Jesus to just touch his little girl so that she would live (5:23). Arriving at the house, He took her by the hand and the dead girl sat up alive (5:41). One His way there, a woman who had bled for twelve years touched His cloak.

Mark 6:5 says He laid His hands on sick people to heal them. He put His fingers in a deaf man's ears (7:33). At Bethsaida people begged Jesus to touch a blind man; He took him by the hand and led him outside the village, where His touch opened the man's blind eyes (8:22). After ordering a demon out of a convulsing boy, Jesus took him by the hand and lifted him to his feet (9:27).

And the One who healed was also the One whose hands expressed love to children. People brought their young ones to Him so that He could touch them. He took them into His arms, put His hands upon them, and blessed them (10:13, 16).

Others had refused to touch many of these people: the dead, the leper, the "unclean" hemorrhaging woman. But their needs were before Him—as obvious as if written on the palms of His hands. He touched to perform miracles. He also touched to tell people that they mattered to Him as flesh-and-blood beings in need of strength, courage, and love.

When we touch, we can offer the same encouraging message. When we grasp the hand of someone who is sick, discouraged, or fearful, that is one way to communicate that they are not forgotten or forsaken. When we join hands to pray, we express that message of spiritual love: "We are one in the Spirit."

Important enough to touch

The appropriate touch may seem like a small thing, but it can mean more than we realize. A dying alcoholic in a large county hospital related how he especially appreciated a certain intern assigned to his floor. What had this young doctor done? He tweaked the patient's toe when he went by. This old, forgotten man was not a chart. He was a real person, and somebody wasn't too important to touch him.

It is particularly true for children that touching affirms the worth. Those who are touched in love—hugged, cuddled, their hair rumpled or stroked, their hands held, their backs rubbed, their shoulders squeezed—are often those who have better self-images and become better adjusted adults.

Several years ago social researchers noted that certain children in an orphanage grew up to be well-adjusted adults while others didn't. When they investigated the situation, they found that the children who had chronic ailments

—who had needed to be picked up and comforted by nurses more often— were the ones who adjusted better later on. Those who had had no physical problems—who had not cried or required much attention—often died early or had personality problems.

I remember how touch broke through a communication barrier one time with my little nephew, who gets lots of hugging and back rubs anyway. One day he came home from kindergarten with one of his "bad day" frowns. Walking aimlessly around the house and hitting furniture, he ran from us when we tried to talk with him. Verbal communication—asking him point blank what was wrong—was futile.

I knew, though, that he loved to have stories read to him. Settling into his father's big, red, velvet rocker, I waved one of his favorite story books and invited him to join me. After one more grumpy circle around the house, he finally climbed up and sat stiffly beside me.

After a few pages I shifted position, wrapped my free arm around his tense little body, and resumed reading. The affirmation of being touched and cared for broke through the communication barrier. Midway through the story he stopped me to explain what had bothered him at school.

Quiet, appropriate touching may reinforce what we communicate verbally. I have noticed how one woman, who is a great encourager to single young career women, will gently take a girl's hand, touch her arm, or place her hand around a girl's waist while they talk. There is nothing offensive in what she does; her mother-like care through touching encourages young women who are away from their own mothers.

The same is true for the elderly. Touching by "substitute" sons and daughters will silently reinforce anything that is said or done. Like the old man who enjoyed having his toe pinched, the elderly appreciate being valued for themselves.

The Latin American ties of many early Wycliffe Bible

translators made the *abrazo*, a big hug, an unofficial greeting world wide among Wycliffe members. (And my short-term service with Wycliffe made me into that type of a hugger.) One day at the headquarters an eighty-nine-year-old retiree who volunteered his time stopped an executive. "I just want to thank you for letting me come to work here at Wycliffe," the elderly man said with deep meaning. They shook hands—then the executive gave him a big *abrazo*. Encouragement. Love.

A wrong touch at the right time

Yet touch can be a very difficult ministry to use appropriately. The nonverbal aspects of our culture abide by certain rules that, when violated, void that communication.

Several years ago I visited an Indian village in rural southern Mexico. I noticed the people greeted me with their hands extended. In typical U.S. response, I grasped their hands for a handshake. They smiled strangely and went their way. Then I noticed how the missionary with me responded. She greeted an Indian friend with a gentle caress on the palm of the hand. I had been enthusiastic, but she had been accurate.

Then on the flight home I saw people hugging the stuffings out of each other at the airport gates. Some were crying—perhaps they had flown home for a funeral. Others were ecstatic in happiness, reunited with loved ones. The touch that would have been inappropriate in that Indian village was acceptable and expected here. They were a different people, a different culture.

To further complicate matters, one culture's "touch rules" may be further altered by the practices of its subcultures. A Greek from New York wouldn't greet a Chinese from San Francisco as he would a fellow Greek. A pro athlete would leave one "touch code" at the soccer field and pick up another "code" to meet the mayor.

As we reach out to others in touch, we must remember that each person may have set certain perimeters for acceptable touching. Or he may have had bad experiences from touching. The memory of a perversion may haunt him.

Touching also can be a difficult method of communication to write about. It's difficult for me because I did not learn until recently to touch freely and lovingly. And for a while I allowed an emotional hurt to make touching repulsive to me. Besides that, the whole realm of touching is hard to describe and recommend. What is right for one person may be wrong for another.

Our culture often sees problems when unrelated men and women touch each other. One pastor warned, for example, that he'd noticed touching between men and women aged thirty-five to forty-five often carried more than innocent, friendly signals. He remembered a woman who greeted him after a sermon with great enthusiasm and appreciation. As they talked she caressed the top side of his hand. Her action bothered him. Just as the "holy kiss" of Paul's time called for the deepest spirituality, so the ministry of touching must have no mistaken messages.

Touching calls for the greatest sensitivity to the situation, the person, and the problem. Yet fear of undefined restrictions should not prevent us from encouraging in this wordless way.

Dr. Arden Almquist, for example, told of visiting a single woman missionary on a field tour On his last night in her town they got together to talk about the work. They were together in a plainly furnished room, sitting across from each other but within arm's length.

He knew this woman had surrendered a romance to remain in missionary service and had gone through some lonely times. As they talked he sensed she had something to say to him.

"The moment came when I felt I would ask her about the friend she had left behind," Almquist recalls. "I had brought up the subject earlier, in a casual way as we walked the streets and had received a casual, tossed reply that dismissed any exploration of her real feelings. This time she seemed ready to struggle with the loneliness her decision had imposed upon her. There was a lengthy silence. Slowly her eyes welled with tears that rolled down her cheek, coalesced in one large drop on her skirt, and lay there—a tiny globe of reflected light, unabsorbed by the heavy, wool fabric.

"I had dropped my gaze during her discomfiture and my eye caught the movement of the falling tear. Instinctively, I reached over and touched my fingertips to where it lay, pressing it lightly into the fabric. At that, she slipped her hand into mine. We squeezed hands softly but firmly, and after a moment withdrew. Then we looked into each other's eyes and exchanged a smile, whereupon she wiped her tears and shortly began to talk.

"I heard from her sometime after my return to the home office. She didn't refer to the gesture that put us in communication, but she spoke of the understanding and love and trust she had received, and the help it had been to her."[19]

In the midst of pain

Probably the greatest need for touching is to encourage those going through painful situations. Then it communicates what words cannot. It affirms our humanity in a way no other communication can.

One young woman, shattered emotionally, remembers how she found her way to friends to seek comfort for her personal pain. The hurt was too deep to talk about. But the wife of the couple silently rubbed the girl's shoulders and hugged her. "That's all I needed," she said later.

A friend of mine who lost her second baby, overdue six weeks and weighing eleven pounds, was told after the difficult delivery that she could bear no more children. A third pregnancy resulted in a miscarriage, bearing out the doctor's prediction. But after prayer she and her husband determined to try once more.

This time, she started to bleed and went to bed to save the baby. When the normal due date arrived, the woman doctor confirmed that the child was ready to be born and said they would induce labor to prevent the baby from going overterm like the other one. As my friend and her husband got to the hospital, a midwestern blizzard blew up, delaying the doctor's arrival.

"When the doctor finally got there," my friend recalled, "I was in the delivery room in the last stages of labor. But my greater pain was concern that this baby would be okay. The doctor, herself a mother, came over and put her hand on my arm. All she said was, 'It sure does hurt, doesn't it?' By that action of touching and acknowledging me, I felt like she was with me, and she was going to go through all of it with me."

The child was born and was normal. And after that my friend had six other children.

Touch also comforts the grieving like nothing else. A pastor came to a parishioner's home after learning of a husband's death. The widow met him at the door and said through tears, "He's with the Lord now. Heaven is so much closer now."

"It was so easy," the pastor says, "to put my arms around her and squeeze her."

The pastor of another church learned that one of his members had accidentally backed a tractor over his two-year-old son and killed him. As the pastor and his wife drove to the family's farm, the question, "What do I say on an occasion like this?" hung in his throat.

"I could think of nothing appropriate," the pastor says, "but when we got there the wife threw her arms around my wife, and I embraced the man and said, 'We've just come to weep with those that weep.' And we did, and that seemed enough. Later there came the right time to talk about what had happened in the light of God's love and sovereign will."[20]

As people work through the grieving process, touch can continue to soothe the ragged edges of sorrow.

On the Mother's Day after my mother's death, I fought tears all through a church service commemorating motherhood. At Sunday school, a friend slid into the chair next to me and said quietly, "Today I want you to know that I care." She slipped her arm around my shoulder. It triggered the tears that I needed to shed—and encouraged me.

A practice, not a ritual

Recognizing the ministry of touch, some churches have attempted to put this form of intimacy into church worship services. One pastor asks people to pray for others during a part of the service and, afterward, to touch someone near them. He even steps down from the pulpit to touch people himself.[21]

He believes it creates an environment of caring.

Perhaps it does, but I believe that we need to guard against touch's becoming a ritualistic, mechanical thing. It's an intimate communication, far more volatile than words on paper or speech. It invades inter-personal distance and fares poorly between strangers.

But there are many whom we could encourage by touching. I admit I am weak in this area and at times have seemed like a cigar store statue. But as the Lord rubs His balm of love into my life, I'm learning how people are consoled or affirmed by the simple act of touching.

So I am trying to shake and squeeze hands more often, to lightly touch arms or shoulders, and to hug. I am trying to be sensitive to times when this nonverbal communication will work a lot better than anything I say or do.

And I try to remember the One whose strong, calloused carpenter's hands healed people, blessed children, and accepted the nails of Roman executioners.

A hymn by Charles Wesley reminds me that

> Before the throne my Surety stands,
> My name is written on His hands.

Touching people—making them whole.

The Encouragement of Mashed Potatoes 7

Be hospitable to one another without complaint. —The apostle Peter (1 Pet. 4:9)

Hot, dusty, and weary from his walk from here to there, the man braced his staff against a wall, untied his sandals and eased his body onto the little cot. He closed his eyes and began to smell fresh, cool air stirring up the hotness of the late afternoon. Sounds of the street clattered below him. Faintly he heard a woman humming as she prepared dinner. She would bring him a tray, then graciously leave so that he could rest.

Not everyone would be so gentle and unobtrusive. Most people entertaining a prophet of God would want the whole world to know and throw a party. But not the Shunammite woman. Her concern, respect, and love had turned a rooftop corner into a private haven where Elisha could be restored on his long walks through the Jezreel plain (2 Kings 4:8-10).

Similar cameos of hospitality are hung throughout Scripture's halls of fame. Sarah, laughing to herself, patted the bread cakes for three mysterious visitors who told her she was going to have a baby (Gen. 18). Jethro took in a lonely vagabond named Moses, and gained a someday-famous son-in-law (Exod. 2:20). An angel turned down Manoah's generous offer of dinner, but left him with an incredible prophecy of a son to be named Samson (Judges 13).

Abigail apologized for her foolish husband and asked David to help himself to the raisins and figs she'd brought (1 Samuel 25). A widow at Zarephath shared with Elijah what she thought was the last meal in her cupboard, and found her pantry adequate while he stayed (1 Kings 17).

For the love of strangers

I once thought it strange how these people outdid themselves for strangers and vagabonds. Then I learned this was a sacred duty among the Israelites. After bondage in Egypt, God told them "the stranger who resides with you shall be to you as the native among you, and you shall love him as yourself" (Lev. 19:34). The Israelites had been strangers themselves in the land of Egypt; now they could be kind to other strangers.

In New Testament times, that duty became a joy when Christians hosted other Christians. Acts records how Paul enjoyed hospitality offered by Lydia and a jailer in Philippi, Jason in Thessalonica, Aquila and Priscilla in Corinth, Philip in Caesarea, and Publius at Malta.

Hospitality was considered so important a Christian virtue that it was required in the résumé of a potential elder or overseer (Titus 1:8 and 1 Tim. 3:2). John's third letter includes a reminder about housing itinerant Christian workers (3 John 5-6). Paul's famous list of Christian behaviors in Romans 12 included hospitality among other debts of love. Paul also advised Timothy that one mark of a godly widow was that she had shown hospitality to strangers (1 Tim. 5:10).

The Greek word for hospitality, *philoxenia*, tells much about its original function. *Philo* refers to "brotherly love" (hence we get "Philadelphia," city of brotherly love). *Xeno* means "strangers" (from the same root that English gets its word "xenophobia," fear of strangers). Putting the two together makes it, literally, "love of strangers." That's why Christians are told in Hebrews 13:2, "Do not neglect to show hospitality to strangers, for by this some have entertained angels without knowing it." Surely this was the case for Sarah! And Peter adds that such service to one another required a positive, loving attitude: "Be hospitable to one another without complaint" (1 Pet. 4:9). Loving hospitality is not an option—it's a command.

For the love of Jesus

When I saw that the New Testament definition of hospitality focused on strangers, I felt guilty inviting friends for a meal and time together. Then I saw that even the Lord Jesus enjoyed simply being with friends. In Bethany, He was welcome enough to use the back door at Mary and Martha's home (Luke 10, John 11). Zaccheus "received Christ gladly" into his home (Luke 19:6). So did others; Jesus was seen eating and visiting with tax gatherers and "sinners" so often that the pinch-nosed Pharisees complained.

I saw how the hospitality offered to Jesus not only allowed Him to relax and just enjoy people, but to extend His base of ministry. And so it could be for me. I could express my love for Jesus by opening my home to others for His sake. That helped me redefine hospitality as this: "I love you so much for Christ's sake that I want to share my haven with you and encourage you. My home and my family are as yours."

That definition of hospitality was fleshed out by others for me many times when I lived in Central Washington with my first job as a newspaper reporter. I was drawn to the pastor's wife, a gregarious, huggable woman who seemed to have a special place in her heart for the church's young single women. I lost count of the meals I shared at their table and the times their family of five squeezed into my tiny apartment for spaghetti.

Our friendship became so close and family-like that one time I dared to experiment on them with an untried recipe for salmon croquettes. The missus asked for the recipe, even though the kids picked at the one croquette they were required to sample. We talked and laughed about my six-year-old goldfish Keith, which had finally died a few days before. And when they left, I found the pastor had written in my guest book: "Dinner was great . . . but are you sure you buried Keith?"

I remember warmly the informal banter and fellowship. But I also have many friends who rarely invite people in. When they do, it's an ordeal. The house has to be immaculate, the dishes set exactly right. By the time the guests come, everybody's unnatural.

At times I have to agree with a missionary friend who remarked: "A lot of people don't invite others over because they think their homes aren't good enough. They're waiting until they get the linoleum laid or they can buy a decent couch. If they'd only realize I don't want to look at their house. I want to enjoy *them*."

Tops on her list of "hospitality" during furloughs was an old farm house where oilcloth covered the table and none of the plates matched. The menu was stew, and the hostess one who rarely took off her oversized apron.

"They just took us in," she said. "We felt right at home. We didn't have to pretend."

Not only did that farm wife feed them and provide beds for the night, but she offered to do their laundry. And the next morning before they left, she packed them a lunch.

Busy hostess? Yes. But not a Martha, that criticized sister of Mary-the-Listener. I think the Lord had a different type of "hostessing" in mind when He rebuked Martha for her house duties. I think He wearied of her *fussing*. He simply wanted her to enjoy having Him there.

That was the situation of a friend's mother who became bedridden and unable to continue hosting a women's Bible study. The woman who taught the study, knowing how much the mother enjoyed having the women over, refused to take it elsewhere. Unable to act as a "Martha," she became a "Mary" as the women continued to come, sometimes holding the study around her bed and putting chairs away afterwards. Even though she couldn't play the hostess role, they still considered her home a haven.

Practicing hospitality as a haven characterizes the lifestyle of two middle-aged women I met at church while attending graduate school. Jinny and Marty, both single, proved to me that marital status is no barrier to being hospitable. They have a large house so that they can sleep and feed guests as they have the opportunity. Beds and couches can accommodate nine and their dining room table opens up to fourteen.

They've opened their home to foreign students at a near-by community college, helping these young people feel welcome through dinners. One Christmas they had twenty-nine in for a holiday party. Overnight guests—friends of friends, often strangers recommended to them—have come from throughout the United States.

"My family never had company when I was a child," recalls Jinny, "so I decided that hospitality was the main thing I wanted to practice when I was an adult. As I grew up and started work, quite a bit of hospitality was shown me by people at church. When I saw what an exciting thing it was—having different people into your home, exposing children to missionaries—I decided that's what I wanted to do."

Marty, who grew up on a farm in Ohio, remembers the church corn roasts that brought out fifty people to her parents' place. But the ministry she and Jinny now carry out is something far more spontaneous. Often they're asked to house people they hardly know.

"A couple days ago we got a call asking if we could help a family that needed overnight accommodations," Jinny recalls. "They were driving from Texas to the Great Lakes

and had to stop here, but because of college commencement all the motels in town were filled. They were so exhausted that they fell asleep on the sofa before dinner. But
they appreciated being able to stay. It takes time for us to
prepare for the company and feed them, but we get the
blessing."

The women prepare for the extra costs of hospitality by
gardening, canning, and freezing to reduce food bills.

"I enjoy people," says Jinny. "I think that too many people are embarrassed to have others in if their house isn't exactly what it should be. If we used that as an excuse we
wouldn't have anybody in. Our place isn't fancy. We have a
lot of second-hand furniture. But we share what we have,
and that's what the Lord wants."

How different the attitude of host and guests the day
Jesus accepted an invitation to eat with one of the leaders of
the Pharisees. Members of the Ph.B.I. (Pharisaical Bureau
of Investigation) hunched in every shadow. They hastily
scribbled notes as Jesus healed a man of dropsy. Surely
there had to be a negative to lay against Him in that! When
the dinner bell clanged, they fought over the places of honor
at the table.

Jesus saw quickly this dinner was deteriorating into a
social show. He'd had enough. Turning to the host, he offered some advice that was about as welcome as a bouquet
of skunk cabbage.

Repayment not needed

"When you give a luncheon or a dinner," Jesus said, "do
not invite your friends or your brothers or your relatives or
rich neighbors, lest they also invite you in return, and repay-
ment come to you. But when you give a reception, invite
the poor, the crippled, the lame, the blind, and you will be
blessed, since they do not have the means to repay you; for

you will be repaid at the resurrection of the righteous" (Luke 14:12-14).

I think Jesus would have included both the physically *and* spiritually poor, crippled, and blind—the sort of people who wouldn't get three-star ratings from the Charming Guest Guild. The person who opened his home to such people wouldn't make the society pages, but the Lord would take note of his mercy.

I was fairly new to town and to my first newspaper job when a severe sore throat was diagnosed as "mono" and I was ordered to bed. I was living alone, several hours' journey from my parents' home, and so weak and sick I could barely pour myself a glass of orange juice. Christian friends, though, learned of my predicament and came and took me to their home. They put me in their daughter's bed (she was away at college) and cared for me until I had enough strength to navigate at home again.

My parents did something similar for the elderly widow who lived across the street. One morning she escaped a fire in her home by rolling down a porch roof, falling into a large hedge. She broke no bones but the fall incapacitated her for a long time. When she was released from the hospital, her house was still under repair. Although she and her late husband were childless, she did have nephews in the area. But none offered to take her in. Neither did friends from the dozen-or-so fraternal organizations she belonged to.

But my parents, who had visited her faithfully in the hospital, turned my old bedroom into her temporary home. I would like to write a happy ending to this story, but I can't. After she got moved back into her home, the woman's age began to tell. Hardening of the arteries, we believed, caused her to become irrational and hostile. As far as we knew, she had never accepted Jesus Christ as her Savior. But through that fire—and the encouragement of hospitality—she did know the love that is possible only through Jesus Christ.

I had my own experience offering hospitality to strangers one winter night after I got home from my newspaper job. The telephone rang and the unfamiliar voice turned out to be a young woman who had written to my weekly women's column.

But this call was not for chitchat. She was down at the city bus station with two of her three children. Her marriage had fallen apart and she was headed to her parents' home. Her transfer bus wouldn't leave until the next morning and the station was closing for the night. She had no money for a motel.

I lived alone in a tiny one-bedroom apartment. But I knew what I had to do. I brought her and the children home, fed them, then opened up my couch (a third-hand relic) and found enough bedding for all of them. I helped rock the frightened children to sleep, then prayed with the mother. On my way to work the next morning, I took them back to the bus depot. I never heard from her again, and perhaps will never know until eternity the rest of her story.

A couple of years later I read Edith Schaeffer's *Hidden Art* and from her chapter on hospitality was challenged again to be ready to show hospitality "even to the least of these" (Matt. 25:40). When her husband was a pastor in an American railroad town many years ago, tramps would come to the parsonage asking, "Cup of coffee, ma'am, and maybe some bread?" Although it was too dangerous to invite a tramp inside (she was alone with children), she rose to the challenge by heating leftover soup and fixing two simple sandwiches. She arranged the snack on an attractive tray with an ivy leaf bouquet and a copy of John's gospel, and served it on the porch.

She told her children that perhaps this kindness would help the man think about the home he once had. And the gospel would give him even more to think about.

We don't have to look for tramps to manifest hospitality

that shows the love of Jesus. One time a teacher who was not a Christian visited a pastor's home to discuss the son's schoolwork. The conversation turned to spiritual things and went on for an hour. During that time the pastor's 14-year-old daughter baked chocolate chip cookies. She brought some out to the father and teacher to snack on. The teacher seemed especially appreciative.

"Later when he went to get his coat and leave," the pastor recalled, "he found a big bag of cookies in his coat pocket with the note, 'Enjoy.' If this man becomes a Christian," he said, "I'm sure my daughter's act of kindness will have been part of it."

Showing hospitality "to the least" should also include those whose lives are fragmented by tragedy. Only those who've gone through the pain of death, great illness, marital struggle or divorce can know the loneliness that these traumas inflict—and, along with that, the physical weakness and digestive problems. People who have hurt deeply often despise the task of cooking or lose their appetites. They feel like the psalmist's description:

> For my days have been consumed in smoke,
> And my bones have been scorched like a hearth.
> My heart has been smitten like grass and withered away,
> Indeed, I forget to eat my bread.
> Because of the loudness of my groaning
> My bones cling to my flesh.
> I resemble a pelican of the wilderness;
> I have become like an owl of the waste places.
> I lie awake,
> I have become like a lonely bird on a housetop
> (Psalm 102:3-7).

I don't know about you, but I'd rather not have a hollow-eyed pelican or owl in my house! And yet Jesus wants us to show special love to the hurting.

The healing of hospitality

When somebody dies, friends often rally with gifts of food to express sympathy and to help with the extra guests. And that's fine. But after the flowers have wilted and the last pan returned, we should seek new ways to show consoling hospitality.

At my parents' memorial services, several said, "Let me know how I can help." But I didn't know what type of help they'd be willing to give and, most of all, I was too shy to contact them. Alone in a town I'd left a decade before, I not only hurt, I was lonely. I started to resemble a pelican of the wilderness as I started poking through possessions to clean out the house.

But then a few called and insisted that I come for dinner with their families. Those home-cooked family meals in another setting—away from the boxfuls of memories—were my oases of consolation. Hospitality helped heal my torn heart.

In my case, I preferred to go to a home rather than a restaurant. Large crowds made me feel even lonelier. When I saw older couples holding hands (as my parents often did in their last years together) I grieved anew. But among friends in a comfortable home, a sense of security shielded me. And I felt the freedom to talk out the hurts that had built up unhealthily.

At college a few years before, however, I was part of a group of "comforters" who chose restaurant fare to show loving hospitality to a friend. Early in February, the boyfriend of a young woman who lived upstairs committed suicide just a few days before the campus sweetheart banquet. Some of us without dates decided to spare this girl the trauma of watching her roommates get ready and go. We snatched her away from campus early and took her to a nice restaurant, then to a sacred concert. Her hurt didn't disappear, of course, but on that difficult night she knew that friends cared.

How much of our "havens" should hospitality invade? One family included me on their vacation—an act of kindness which continues to amaze and touch me. Early one summer my emotions and hopes were torn apart when a romance I thought was leading to marriage abruptly dissolved. Earlier that year, I'd scheduled my annual vacation with a summer honeymoon in mind. I took the breakup hard and despaired over what to do with that vacation time. I needed to get away but, as I remember, my parents had left for an overseas vacation. I felt imprisoned by my broken dreams.

My pastor's family, who had followed closely this hopeful romance, shared my hurt. So much so in fact, that they invited me to join their family of five on a vacation to Yellowstone Park. Of course, I contributed to their trip costs. But I was more than repaid by their surrogate family love.

Creative hospitality allows encouragement to work both ways. One time I lived in an apartment with no laundry facilities and soon wearied of trips to the laundromat. About that time a widow in my church whom I called "Grandma G" invited me to use her washer and dryer. I hastily accepted, suggesting we potluck our leftovers on wash nights to double a chore with a dinner visit.

For her laundry room I bought a novelty piggy bank and plunked there the quarters I would otherwise have paid at the laundromat.

The arrangement put chicken feed in her purse and gave her someone to talk to. We both got a good meal and a break from our own leftovers. As our friendship grew and our conversations deepened, I got godly counsel from a woman who encouraged and loved me.

Over mashed potatoes—and yogurt and eggplant and homemade applesauce—our souls were mutually refreshed.

A Little Field Work

Contributing to the needs of the saints . . . .
—The apostle Paul (Rom. 12:13)

Financial pressures make some people look like they're dieting on lemons. But that wasn't true of a college friend, Lorraine. It only took a couple of classes before one professor nicknamed her "Laughing Woman." You *had* to smile when you were around her.

But one morning she looked in the mirror in no mood to laugh. An abscessed tooth had puffed her face and she needed professional help, fast.

"You'll need a root canal, cap, crown," the dentist announced as he pulled his instruments out of her mouth.

"How long will it take?" Lorraine mumbled.

"A couple of months."

"What will it cost?"

"About five hundred dollars."

Lorraine melted in dismay. She had no insurance and was scrambling homework and a part time job to get through graduate school. Finances were lean at home too for her widowed mother and two sisters—one a missionary and the other married with a new baby.

The treatment would involve two dentists. One agreed to take payments at ten dollars a month. She could handle that. But the other insisted that his bill (it would come to $305) be paid in full within ninety days.

"I decided the only way I could pay that bill was to work

extra hard and earn extra money," Lorraine says. "But the prospect of doing that—while still keeping up at school—became a burden."

A month after starting treatments, she went to a Christian student retreat where studies on "community" hit hard. Rather than bear her burden alone, she decided to present the "community" of Christian students with her need. On Sunday, the last day, she asked friends to pray that she'd develop a better attitude toward the dentist demanding immediate payment.

"Afterwards," she recallls, "one of the students asked me what I'd do if somebody gave me the money. I laughed and said I'd take it."

Not long after that, while the group waited to eat, she noticed a folded piece of paper labeled with her name. She opened it and found five dollars with an unsigned note specifying the money was for her teeth. When the group regathered she told them about the gift and said, "This starts my tooth fund."

That night at home, a classmate who attended another church called. This friend's Sunday school class had passed the plate and collected $102 for Lorraine.

"Nobody there knew me," Lorraine says. "She said they gave because I was another believer in need. That got me thinking about ways I could help people. I didn't have the finances to share, but I could type, drive, or be a listener."

That Monday Lorraine had another appointment with the dentist who wanted immediate payment. After her treatment she laid sixty dollars (from the $107 she'd received Sunday) in front of the dentist's receptionist.

The woman remarked in surprise, "We thought you had no money."

"I didn't," Lorraine replied, "but I have very special friends who care for me."

She still had $47 left but would eventually owe that dentist

$245 *more*. The next day she found a thick envelope in her campus mailbox.

"When I slit it open I found a huge wad of dollars," she said. "I started to count out five twenties. A girl nearby looked over and remarked, 'That's a lot of money.' I was astounded. I went into the student union where I could count the rest in privacy. That envelope contained two hundred dollars. I was shaking and crying. I needed $245 to pay off my bill and now I had $247. In forty-eight hours after I'd shared my need I had all the money necessary to pay the dentist!"

An anonymous note had been tucked in with that envelope of money, citing Acts 4:32-35.

> Not one of them claimed that anything belonging to him was his own; but all things were common property to them. . . . there was not a needy person among them, for all who were owners of land or houses would sell them and bring the proceeds of the sales, and lay them at the apostles' feet; and they would be distributed to each, as any had need.

At her last dental appointment, Lorraine announced to the dentist and receptionist, "I want you to know that I can pay you off. I believe God takes care of us and one of the ways He does this is through people who believe in Him."

The dentist was amazed as she handed over the money. The receptionist said, "Boy, your friends really love you."

"At that point it hit me." Lorraine says now. "My friends really *do* love me."

Later an income tax refund paid most of the balance due the other dentist who had been willing to wait for his fee. But for Lorraine that zero balance receipt from the first dentist became her testimony of God's supply and His people's love.

The spirit of generosity that encouraged Lorraine was the same seen in Barnabas, whose first act recorded by Scripture was the encouragement of finances. Acts 4:37 tells how he sold his tract of land and laid the proceeds at the apostles' feet to be used for the needy.

Prideful giving spells disaster

But right on the heels of his gift came one from a couple whose giving showed another motive. Luke hints that they were different by using the conjunction "but."

> But a certain man named Ananias, with his wife Sapphira, sold a piece of property, and kept back some of the price for himself, with his wife's full knowledge, and bringing a portion of it, he laid it at the apostles' feet (Acts 5:1-2).

Ananias and Sapphira had some attitude problems. If you planted a rock garden by your fire hydrant, they were the types to turn their front yard into a replica of the grounds of Forest Lawn. Or when you put hamburgers on your barbecue grill, they put steak on theirs—and made sure the wind was blowing in your direction.

When they saw Barnabas donate one hundred percent of his real estate transaction to the church's emergency fund, they figured they could easily top his price. Perhaps their talk at dinner went like this:

Ananias (waving check): Sapphira, you'll never believe what I got for that lot at Third and Main, you know, the one we were going to sell for the church.

Sapphira (eyes bulging): Boy, what a stack!

Ananias (frowning): Sure could use some of this myself.

Sapphira: You're right. Darling, you know that cute little garden cart I saw in Omar's window?

Ananias: Yeah, it wouldn't hurt to hold back just a little. Nobody will know. We'll just tell them it's the whole business and everybody will admire us for being so sacrificial. Can't let that Barney get one up on us.

Sapphira: That's right, Ananias; they'll never know.

Acts 5 tells what happened. God knew. The part they lied

about and kept back for themselves barely paid for their funerals.

Giving is a godly exercise. But it can also become a snare for pride. Jesus said:

> When therefore you give alms, do not sound a trumpet before you, as the hypocrites do in the synagogues and in the streets, that they may be honored by men. Truly I say to you, they have their reward in full. But when you give alms, do not let your left hand know what your right hand is doing that your alms may be in secret; and your father who sees in secret will repay you (Matt. 6:2-4).

Giving out of wealth and poverty

Perhaps Paul was thinking of God's death judgment on this couple when he wrote Timothy to instruct the rich "to be generous and ready to share" (1 Tim. 6:18). He also wrote the Romans that part of the nitty-gritty of the Christian walk was "contributing to the needs of the saints" (Rom. 12:13). When we read Paul's doctrinal letters I think we fail to realize how often he was involved in delivering financial gifts from one church to another. And how often financial encouragement came addressed to him. The book of Philippians includes a thank-you for such a gift.

The New Testament suggests that churches that gave to help another were sometimes worse off than the churches that received. The Macedonians, for example, weren't living on Fifth Avenue. Yet in giving to the Corinthians, Paul noted, "in a great ordeal of affliction their abundance of joy and their deep poverty overflowed in the wealth of their liberality" (2 Cor. 8:2).

We need to realize this to understand that the ministry of encouraging through money and material goods needn't be limited to the wealthy. True, God has blessed some people with wealth and they turn it right back to Him. We can learn from their attitudes. R. G. LeTourneau was an engineering and machinery genius who made millions. Besides establishing a Christian college, he reportedly gave ninety percent of his income to the Lord's work. He once remarked, "The question is not how much of my money I give to God, but rather how much of God's money I keep for myself."[22]

The same was true of Maxey Jarman, who built a billion-dollar corporation, Genesco, from a company of seventy-five employees. When reverses came, he continued to contribute generously to Christian ministries. Even at the lowest point of his personal fortune, he gave away the inheritance from his mother's estate to Christian causes.

Fred Smith, Jarman's friend and colleague over four decades, once asked him, during the darkest days of his temporary financial crunch, whether he ever thought of the millions he had given away.

"Of course I have," Jarman replied, "but remember I didn't lose a penny I gave away. I only lost what I kept."[23]

Giving demonstrates God's power and planning. There may be times we won't know that what we are prompted to give fills exactly a need known only to God. Giving can encourage both those who give and those who receive.

I remember one man who signed a mission "faith pledge" for one hundred dollars a month. This meant he expected God to supply one hundred dollars a month—twelve hundred dollars a year—above his regular giving to support a certain mission. It was an incredible sum to consider since he was retired and had barely enough with his pension to support himself and his wife.

The first year of the "faith pledge," the funds came in when a company called him out of retirement to work on a special project. The next year he made an identical "faith pledge," then his leg was amputated and he couldn't work. It appeared there was no way he could meet the pledge.

But while he recuperated he realized he could no longer

drive his little foreign car. Two legs were required to operate its manual transmission. And his wife couldn't drive. He placed an ad in the paper, sold the car for twelve hundred dollars and met his pledge!

The specifics of His care

On their 1966 furlough near Chicago, my missionary friend Helen and her husband struggled with a shrinking support check. They were down to five hundred dollars a month to house and feed their family of eight children. More than two hundred dollars of that was taken up with rent and utilities.

"At that time we had a lot of friends from nearby states come visit us and see Chicago," Helen recalls. "It seemed that people were coming and going as fast as we could change the bedsheets. With all this company there were extra expenses. Yet in April our support check dropped to $325.

"We asked, 'Lord! What's going on?' It seemed His Name was on the line. We could barely feed our own family, let alone guests. Then we learned that a family that had not been in favor of what we were doing wanted to visit us—that month!"

The morning before their arrival Helen collected the family wash to take to the laundromat. She had just enough coins to run the machines. As she dressed her preschoolers she heard a knock at the door. There stood a church friend, her nightgown visible beneath her coat.

"While I was ironing my husband's shirt," the woman said, "the Lord told me to bring this over to you right away. I hope you're not offended."

She handed Helen a used envelope apparently pulled in haste from a wastebasket. Inside was fifteen dollars, just enough for food for the weekend guests.

"The family came and never knew there was a problem," Helen says.

During the Depression one man came to the end of his first year at college without his bill paid. The registrar would not allow him to take his last test to finish the year until he had paid up. He only owed seventy-five dollars, "but in those days it was like two thousand dollars today," he says. "It was a horrendous amount of money to me. I was puzzled why God would bring me to school and then desert me at the last moment."

The morning the balance was due, he received seventy-five dollars from a Christian in another state who didn't even know he needed exactly that amount.

At Bible school I frequently shared friends' amazement when checks or anonymous envelopes of money appeared in their mailboxes for tuition or personal needs. One time a roommate needed new glasses and anonymously received $83.59—in cash—with a note signed "Romans 12:13." She looked it up and read, "Contributing to the needs of the saints." The amount covered all but a few dollars of her optometrist's bill.

Making giving special

Encouraging through giving can also be a creative ministry. One family decides together who needs special financial help. Then the children help leave anonymous envelopes of money on car seats or other places where the people will find it.

But people appreciate, too, knowing the source of the encouragement. I remember shaking hands with a man while I was raising support for mission service. To my shock the wad of paper he slipped into the handshake was a large-denomination bill.

Later during my mission service, a couple in a rural area

sent a check with this note: "The Lord gave us a good weekend at a little fruit stand we put up by the road. Here's the Lord's part and we want it for you." I knew they lived with limited means; their sacrifice was a sweet fragrance in my life.

One time a seminary student heard of another's urgent need for cash. He had no money to spare. But overcome with love and concern for his friend, he sold his stereo sound system—his prized hobby—and gave his friend the money.

But we shouldn't limit the definition of "giving" to money. Sometimes our resources or material goods, such as food or supplies, can help encourage someone just as well. I've been encouraged by gifts of fabric and clothing, home canning and garden vegetables, and even a spare mattress. I've been encouraged, too, by loans. One weekend friends handed me the keys to their second car so I'd have transportation to move.

The late Henrietta Mears, teacher of the large college Sunday school class at Hollywood Presbyterian Church, encouraged some of her seminary students by buying them their first "preacher's suits" and winter overcoats. She told them to think of these gifts simply as loans and that someday they could do the same for others.[24]

Author James L. Johnson remembers how a loan of money encouraged him in his writing career when he was a 20-year-old Navy veteran starting junior college.

"I had to write everything in longhand and I was getting so frustrated," he recalls. "I really needed a typewriter."

When his sister suggested that he ask Matt, the neighborhood grocer, for a loan, Johnson was reluctant. He knew Matt had little profit to spare. Finally his sister's urging got to him and he ran over to the store.

"Matt, I need a loan of sixty-five dollars for a typewriter," Johnson blurted. "I just can't write without a typewriter, so let me sign a note and I'll pay you back."

"I trust you," the old grocer said as he handed the amount over to Johnson. Johnson bought the typewriter the next day and repaid the grocer with his next G.I. check.

"Matt didn't know how much that loan meant to me," Johnson says now. "Getting that typewriter and seeing words come out in print on paper broke me out of my shell. I used that typewriter for years. I hated to part with it."

Besides gifts or loans, I see a third way that giving can encourage others. Perhaps it doesn't quite fit into this chapter. Maybe it's more a "booster shot"—a message that a person is important to someone else. But it does require reaching into our financial resources.

It's a gray March day as I edit this chapter, but somebody has given me sunshine for my room. Yesterday, by air mail, came a box of fresh daffodils from my home in Puyallup, Washington. A gal I knew at church there, out of her love, bought and sent me an early spring to encourage me.

When I was working as "temporary help" I noticed how one woman was gloomy over family problems and sour and sharp around co-workers. Then one morning the door near her desk opened and a friend shyly glided a potted plant onto her desk.

"Just want you to know we love you," the friend said, hugging her and then leaving quickly. The worker was overwhelmed and dug in her purse hastily for a hanky. But the rest of that week I noticed a definite turnaround in her attitude. She'd been encouraged.

Midway through my graduate program, my heavy study and work schedule had pushed me to my emotional limits. Then one day I was mystified by a package slip in my mailbox. Bushel-big, but weighing only a few pounds, it turned out to be a "care" package of cookies and teas from my sister's family. A sign on top (in my niece's best third-grade penmanship) said "Survival Kit For Aunt Jeanne."

And the packaging material, which encouraged me as much as anything, was hundreds of plastic foam disks on which the niece and nephew had drawn "happy faces."

Scripture tells how the righteous man is a generous and giving one. The psalmist said:

I have been young, and now I am old;
Yet I have not seen the righteous forsaken,
Or his descendants begging bread.
All day long he is gracious and lends;
And his descendants are a blessing (Psalm 37:25-26).

And over in Proverbs:

The righteous gives and does not hold back (21:26).
He who gives to the poor will never want,
But he who shuts his eyes will have many curses (28:27).

Even the virtuous woman stretched out her hands to the needy: (Prov. 31:20).

Paul suggested a good rehabilitation program for a thief was being given the responsibility for someone in financial need: "Let him who steals steal no longer; but rather let him labor, performing with his own hands what is good, in order that he may have something to share with him who has need" (Eph. 4:28).

James said feeding or clothing the brother or sister in need was proof of our faith (James 2:14-26).

Encouraging by giving reminds us that we're only custodians of our material resources. And giving not only proves our faith, it also builds our faith and that of others.

Just ask Lorraine—and she'll show you the tooth that somebody's love crowned and capped.

No Feet Too Grubby 9

*He who sees a need and waits to be asked for help is
as unkind as if he had refused it.* —Dante[25]

Several years ago some researchers decided to find out if
good seminarians were also good Samaritans. At Princeton
Seminary they selected forty ministerial students under the
pretense of doing a survey on careers in the church. They
asked each student to walk to a nearby building to dictate an
impromptu talk into a tape recorder. Some were told to talk
on the good Samaritan; some, of their concerns for a career.

What the seminarians didn't know was that there would
be another test as they walked to the building. The researchers had planted an actor who, as a seminarian approached,
would groan and slump to the ground.

More than half of the students walked right on by, the researchers reported. "Some, who were planning their disser-
tation on the good Samaritan," the researchers added,
"literally stepped over the slumped body as they hurried
along."[26]

How different the attitude of someone to whom the New
Testament devotes only four verses. His name, Onesiphorus,
meant "bringer of profit" but more accurately he
brought encouragement to Paul in a Roman prison.

Of this man Paul wrote, "Onesiphorus . . . often refreshed
me, and was not ashamed of my chains; but when he was in
Rome, he eagerly searched for me, and found me. . . and
you know very well what services he rendered at Ephesus"

(2 Tim. 1:16-18).

The story behind the story—as best as the pieces can be patched—is that Onesiphorus, hearing of Paul's imprisonment, determined to go help him. He caught a ship out of Ephesus (in today's Turkey), landed in Italy, and walked or caught a wagon up to Rome. Then he had to find a needle in Rome's haystack. Rome had probably six hundred thousand prisoners and was full of dirty holes to store them. Finding Paul wasn't that easy. Nor was ministering to Paul any fun. The jails and dungeons were literally the pits.

What did Onesiphorus do?

That, too, is conjecture. Besides visiting Paul, he probably tended to the apostle's physical needs. Perhaps he brought some better food, washed Paul's clothes, or helped him clean his cell. Maybe he even gave him a haircut or scouted the markets for some more writing paper.

Whatever he did, it took initiative to come. It took courage to be associated with a prisoner. It took the attitude that no feet were too grubby to wash, no person too lowly to help, no job too unpleasant to perform for the sake of Christ. Onesiphorus loved Paul, as the apostle John would later describe love, not with word or tongue only but in deed and truth (1 John 3:18).

Caring enough to serve

People who care enough to help get few headlines. But such people Paul must have had in mind when he wrote the Christians at Corinth: "Those members of the body, which we deem less honorable, on these we bestow more abundant honor, and our unseemly members come to have more abundant seemliness. God has so composed the body, giving more abundant honor to that member which lacked" (1 Cor. 12:23-24).

Jesus said the measure of our greatness in God's kingdom

would be our servanthood (Matt. 20:26-28). He demonstrated His own willingness to be the servant of all when He rose from His most important dinner and went from foot to foot with a basin and towel. Even the traitor's rough, calloused feet felt the cool water and gentle blotting by the Savior's hands.

But a servant attitude—doing the simple things for one another—doesn't come easily. We claim rights to our time and resources and jealously guard them.

A young mother, for example, panicked when her child fell and cut his head. As blood quickly ran over his face, she phoned the first person she could think of: a Christian neighbor. Could she come for a minute to help her determine how serious the cut was? No, the woman replied, she was in the middle of fixing dinner.

A far cry from encouragement.

German pastor Dietrich Bonhoeffer, martyred by the Nazis in 1945, has some who disagree with parts of his theology. But he said critical things about how Christians need to live together.

In his book *Life Together*, he said Christians need to learn how to manifest "active helpfulness" or "simple assistance in trifling, external matters. There is a multitude of these things whenever people live together. Nobody is too big for the meanest service. One who worries about the loss of time that such petty, outward acts of encouragement entail is usually taking the importance of his own career too solemnly."[27]

A challenge to help others also comes from the life of a Frenchman of the sixteenth century whom we know as Brother Lawrence. When he entered a religious community near Paris he was assigned to serve in the kitchen. The task was low, humbling, grubby—but Brother Lawrence found delight in the menial because he had learned to "practice the presence of God" in all things. "I am pleased," he said, "when I can take a straw from the ground simply for the love of God."

Bonhoeffer said it shouldn't be much different for Christians: "In the monastery his vow of obedience to the abbot deprives the monk of the right to dispose of his own time. In the evangelical community life, free service to one's brother takes the place of the vow. Only where hands are not too good for deeds of love and mercy in everyday helpfulness can the mouth joyfully and convincingly proclaim the message of God's love and mercy."[28]

Jesus excluded no one from the ministry of helping. When He talked about His second coming and the final judgment, He said He'd welcome to heaven those who gave Him food when He was hungry, a drink when He was thirsty, and clothing when He was naked. He added that these acts of help and mercy were done to Him when done to others. "Truly I say to you, to the extent that you did it to one of these brothers of Mine, even the least of them, you did it to Me" (Matt. 25:40).

The needs around us

At times needs of others—as they did for the Good Samaritan (and his infamous contemporaries)—will almost fall at our feet. We don't have to look far to find those who need something done but lack the ability. Or those unable to cope with their circumstances due to illness, death, or physical or emotional handicap.

Helping may involve our area of expertise. My father delighted in working at what we called his "tinker bench," where he took apart broken things and put them back together whole. Often he did small repairs for neighbors. And he had a special corner in his heart for older widows in our town. When the elderly widow across the street had to have part of her home rebuilt after a fire, he went over and offered to do things the insurance wouldn't cover. He found a carpet on sale and by cutting carefully was able to give her a rug in her odd-shaped living room.

My mother sewed. She could shape designer-look clothes out of bargain remnants and often sewed for others and their children. Frustrated friends who brought her their sewing problems knew that she could solve them in minutes. For her, fixing a bad zipper was as easy as cracking an egg.

I learned my "expertise" was giving simple haircuts, after roommates noticed me trimming my own hair and asked me to trim theirs. During my second week at Bible school, word of this freebie barber somehow got to the guys. The school had a haircut code and the student body president was one of the first to be told his all-summer grow-out job wouldn't do. He called. I cut. He bragged. And the shaggies lined up—fifty that year.

Often, helping requires only the skills we use every day. A friend, Paula, encouraged me by her willingness to "ride shotgun" (that's what she called it) when I moved from Washington state to Los Angeles to serve with Wycliffe Bible Translators.

I'm not much for driving long distances alone. I have some empathy for Leah—Jacob's weak-eyed wife (Gen. 29:17)—because my eyes turn a patriotic red-white-and-blue after a couple of hours on the freeway. I couldn't imagine twelve hundred miles of it alone, nursing a small rental trailer, too.

But Paula, a single woman in my church, switched her vacation schedule around and helped me drive down. It halved the driving and of course eased my parents' worries.

And who says helping can't be fun? Our laughter helped break the tension as I anticipated the search for housing in a strange town and adjustments to a new job. The first laughs came when Paula turned on the radio and I realized she was twirling the knob to country western. I threatened to uncase my violin (on top of the pile in the back seat) and enlighten her with a Bach concerto.

If one "shotgun" stint wasn't enough, Paula volunteered to help me drive *back* two years later when my short-term service ended. Another two years later, she was along for a move to Illinois. I was encouraged to have her along—especially knowing that she was better at changing flats!

Paula's encouragement cost her her vacation time. But often the bits of time we fritter away daily can be put to use to encourage others. Church people in California spent time writing out the Bible in pencil for a young woman afflicted with a rare disease that left her allergic to nearly everything, including the ink in her Bible.

At another place, college students and friends devoted hours to "patterning" and exercising the limbs of a brain-damaged child. One woman learned Braille so she could label a blind friend's canned foods.

Encouraging can also cost us time plus gas—to help those who are looking for a place to live or work, who need to get out to shop or go to the doctor, or who need errands run for them.

Helping assertively

One woman, wobbly from the flu, had no idea how she'd muster the strength to clean her house before company came. Her neighbor somehow sensed her panic, grabbed a broom and a bucket of cleaning supplies, and knocked at the door.

"I'm Huldah," the helper-neighbor said in a phony accent, grinning. "You 'av yost vun a vree ofternun ov cleaning sorvice." The sick woman was embarrassed momentarily but grateful. After they both laughed, "Huldah" got to work.

One single college student picked up "help" signals from a young mother of two preschoolers, pregnant with her third. The student told her that her next class-free day was to be

"Diana Day" and that she would come over and do housework for her—for free. And the student kept her word, spending the day cleaning an oven, ironing and vacuuming for the mother.

Another time an elderly lady who couldn't do any heavy housework asked Diana how she could help. "Hold the babies," Diana quickly replied. So, doing what comes naturally to grandmothers, the woman freed Diana to go about her work.

One teenager who had a steady babysitting job with a family of two preschoolers knew the mother would often need time away but couldn't afford it. Sometimes she would call the mother and say, "I'd like to take the kids to the park—and this is for free."

Family members can encourage one another by sharing chores. In one farm home the oldest daughter had dish duty—the old-fashioned way—after a late dinner for company and the family of seven. As she tied on her apron, the father came in and said, "Come on, I'll help you and we'll sing."

Those facing a terminal illness or death in the family may appreciate a loving aggressiveness by helpers. It's fine to express concern and sympathy by saying, "Let me know if I can do anything to help," but few will follow up on vague offers. Specifics, however, can encourage.

Joe Bayly remembers the unobtrusive helpfulness of a family friend, a teacher, when their five-year-old was diagnosed as having leukemia.

"When we brought our son home from the hospital," Bayly says, "Lorraine came in every afternoon about six o'clock, said hello to us, and then headed for the kitchen. She did the evening dishes so the whole family could be together in the aftermath of supper. It was a great act of kindness because it allowed us to have our Bible reading and prayer together."[29]

For another family whose father had leukemia, people helped by mowing the lawn, planting a garden, and cleaning the carpets, all without charge.

When death strikes, many help and encourage by bringing food, doing dishes and light housekeeping, taking laundry, babysitting, and providing transportation. But the true encourager also looks for ways to help *after* the funeral, when the impact of death's changes really rocks the grieving.

The week after my father's death, a newlywed friend, Judy, called long distance and asked what practical way she could help me. She insisted on coming so finally I told her the only jobs I could offer her were dull, unpleasant ones—going through my parents' clothes and sorting out a cluttered hobby room. Judy cooked meals ahead for her husband, boarded a bus, and came for five days. Chores that quickly exhausted my tattered patience, she did cheerfully. And she helped me laugh—needed therapy for those sad, lonely days.

A few months later another friend, Ellen, came for a few days—again insisting on helping me with the "grubby jobs"—and helped me clean out a dusty storage shed and some long-forgotten cupboards.

Renewing my parents' house with paint before selling it was another task that overwhelmed me. I started painting the rooms alone, my only comfort a Christian radio station. Several times a day I would have to lie down—the exertion of painting too much for me. But one day a friend who had the morning off came over and helped roll paint on one of the large living room walls. Our talking and singing lightened my load and it became the easiest day of the whole paint task.

Another part of my "cleanout" was holding garage sales to dispose of my parents' things. One neighbor, Ruth, took the initiative to help me set up tables in the garage and also coached me on pricing policies. I had to hold seven sales and she came over the first part of each to help me when the crowds were the largest.

It was no easier for her, emotionally, than it was for me—she had been close to my parents—but she helped with quiet cheerfulness. She reminded me of Romans 12:8, "He who shows mercy, with cheerfulness."

I've heard of churches that sponsor a labor exchange—a man who can do plumbing, for example, will fix a bad sink in exchange for a mechanical job of equal difficulty on his car. But true helping goes beyond the idea of exchange. It is offered without price. Onesiphorus presented no bill to Paul for "prison services." Servanthood demands no wages nor recognition of one's "sacrifice." Jesus washed feet.

I was told of a married student at a seminary who had continually struggled with deadlines. His thesis came due—and overdue—again. Finally the school would give him no more extensions. The night before it was due he found he simply would not be able to get it typed before the deadline. With regret he called the professor, hoping for just one more extension.

"I'm sorry," the professor responded, "I will not give you a further extension." The student was crushed. "But," the professor went on, "if you bring it over to the house tonight I will type it for you." The professor, who also had a family and little spare time, typed that night and into the next day—simply to help the student.

Servanthood evangelism

When helping goes beyond the circles of our family and Christian friends, it shows the love of Jesus in a way people can't forget. The story of the good Samaritan often focuses on the heartlessness of the religious types who walked by the wounded man and the great heart of the Samaritan who helped him. But did you ever think about the wounded guy?

After the snub by his own kin, he was a prime candidate for conversion to Samaritanism—at least he had seen something very beautiful in one of that stripe.

In one church a woman who was a Christian had married a doctor who was very antagonistic to the church and to the Christian faith. The doctor loved his wife enough to bring her to church on Sundays and to pick her up. But he never came in. The pastor made a point of being outside to greet him, but the doctor was always hostile.

Then two things happened. First, the doctor's home was badly damaged by fire. When the pastor went and talked with the man and his family, he offered the church's assistance. Several churchwomen came over to help them clean up and wash walls. Next the doctor's son developed an acute case of asthma and bronchitis. The boy became so sick that the doctor feared he would have to leave his practice and relocate in another area. In his despair the doctor consented to a luncheon appointment with the pastor.

"I think he figured I'd land all over him for not coming to church," the pastor recalled. "It took a while for him to relax at that lunch. But I just told him that the people in the church were very concerned for his boy and family. And I promised to pray for his situation. I didn't preach at him."

From that point, the doctor softened. He asked the pastor to join him for golf. They played and talked, and a friendship grew as the pastor expressed a desire to know about the doctor's work. The doctor then began to show an interest in the church and finally attended a service with his wife. One night at home, within a month after his first visit to the church, he made a profession of faith in Christ.

"We didn't pressure him," the pastor said. "We were simply there, to help when the family needed help, to care. We saw them as people and not as prospects."

Something similar happened after the apostle Paul dropped in at Corinth. Every synagogue where his feet touched the doorway, Jews and Greeks were stirred up as he preached that Jesus was the Christ.

But the Jews started to fume and labeled him a heretic. Finally, shaking his coat, he stormed, "Your blood be upon your own heads! I am clean. From now on I shall go to the Gentiles" (Acts 18:6). He took up new headquarters in a home next door to the synagogue. Crowds continued to listen and the synagogue leader Crispus, along with his entire family, received Christ. Of course, that meant Crispus lost his job as synagogue leader. He was succeeded by a fellow named Sosthenes.

A year and a half went by and the tempers of the Jews grew hotter. Finally they hauled Paul into the outdoor Greek court, but the judge stated icily that religious controversies weren't in his line of duty. He ordered them to leave.

Frustrated and inflamed, they grabbed Sosthenes on the way out and furiously beat him up while the judge looked the other way.

Nothing more is said about this hapless fellow until 1 Corinthians 1:1, where Paul begins this letter, "Paul, called as an apostle of Jesus Christ by the will of God, and Sosthenes our brother." Apparently this man was the second leader that this Corinthian synagogue had lost to Christ! How that happened is not told.

Could it have been "encouragement evangelism"? I'm guessing that the enraged crowd dissipated into the city while the bruised, helpless man lay bleeding. Perhaps Paul was nearby, safe with one of the judge's guards, and when the crowd left, rushed over to Sosthenes and with some friends carried him to help. Perhaps they went to the home of Aquila and Priscilla, mentioned at the beginning of the chapter (Acts 18:2). Maybe Luke the doctor also tended the man's injuries.

I believe Sosthenes became the object of helping and caring from some people who by all rights should have—like the Levite and the priest in the story of the good Samaritan—passed on the other side of the road. Sosthenes couldn't resist the quality of thier lives, and eventually he couldn't resist embracing Jesus as Savior.

Paul said we should exhibit in our lives the attitude of Jesus, "who, although He existed in the form of God, did not regard equality with God a thing to be grasped, but emptied himself, taking the form of a bondservant" (Phil. 2:6-7).

Helping people says, "You are important enough to me for me to serve you. I do not consider myself too good for you."

One more thing about people who stoop in love to wash grubby feet: they're already in the proper posture for worshiping a King.

Epaphras and His Kin 10

A Christian fellowship lives and exists by the intercession of its members for one another, or it collapses. —Bonhoeffer[30]

They weren't the original Hardy boys, but hardy they were. We'll call them Danny, Hank, Mike, and Ozzie. Innocents abroad, they'd been snatched up in a war and marched off to a special school to be retrained for the conqueror's service.

They could have melted into the walls and gotten along fine. But they had one problem. Their masters had a different religion that required compromising their standards. When junk food came on the menu, for example, they won a concession for vegetables and water. But each objection was a risk. Their top boss was a scandalously cruel man named Neb—not the type you'd want for a next-door neighbor. To him, killing was a form of recreation.

Drop the nicknames and maybe the story will come into focus: Daniel, Hananiah, Mishael and Azariah (in Babylon they were renamed Belteshazzar, Shadrach, Meshach, and Abed-nego). These four youths, captured in Israel, were about as out-of-place in Nebuchadnezzar's palace as lilies might be in a wrecking yard.

Strengthened by their mutual faith in God, they'd made it—so far.

Then one night Nebuchadnezzar's head swam with an incredible nightmare. He summoned his local dream experts and, without revealing it, ordered an interpretation. Despite all their recipes for frog stew, these seers were baffled. Nebuchadnezzar got angry. His hood men started sharpening their swords and Daniel and his three buddies were among those on the hit list.

Daniel knew he had only one option: in the power of the Lord of Hosts he would have to try to interpret the secret dream. It seemed impossible. But look at what he did.

> So Daniel went in and requested of the king that he would give him time, in order that he might declare the interpretation to the king. Then Daniel went to his house and informed his friends, Hananiah, Mishael and Azariah, about the matter, in order that they might request compassion from the God of heaven concerning this mystery, so that Daniel and his friends might not be destroyed with the rest of the wise men of Babylon (Dan. 2:16-18).

See that phrase, "request compassion"? That means *pray*. The same man who would later face opposition for praying three times a day to God (Dan. 6:10) knew that saints advance on their knees. And he could count on his friends to be prayer partners for an emergency that put God's honor at stake.

The rest of chapter 2 is good news. God told Daniel the dream and its interpretation. Daniel astonished Nebuchadnezzar by revealing it. And all four got promotions.

The encouragement of another's prayers

I appreciate this incident from the life of Daniel for illustrating how we should pray for one another. It shows the mighty power of the Father to respond to the prayers of His children. It also suggests the consistent attitude of caring by praying. I doubt if the emergency over the king's dream was the first time these four prayed together. I think they must have gathered often to uphold each other and to encourage each other in a difficult situation far from home.

The body that weeps and rejoices together is the body that prays together. Scripture commands that we get so involved in each others' lives that their needs occupy our prayer time.

> First of all, then, I urge that entreaties and prayers, petitions and thanksgivings, be made on behalf of all men (1 Tim. 2:1).

When I first really considered that list, my writer-editor instinct wanted to reduce those four similar words for "prayer" to one. But when I hauled out some study aids and dug into the Greek, I was convicted by the richness of that instruction and the poverty of my own prayers for others.

The first two words, "entreaties" and "prayers," are similar in meaning. "Entreaties" comes from the Greek *deesis,* which designates a prayer for wants or needs, such as Zacharias's and Elizabeth's petition for a son (Luke 1:13). "Prayers" is from *proseuche,* and refers to general prayer— the act of talking to God. Jesus told His disciples, "And everything you ask in prayer (*proseuche),* believing, you shall receive" (Matt. 21:22).

But that third word, "petitions," cuts deeper into the concept of praying for others. It comes from *enteuxis,* a term for the boldness and freedom of approaching a king with a request for others. When we intercede, we come before the throne of the heavenly King asking for others' needs, bold and free because of our status as heirs through Jesus Christ.

Somehow I had never quite fit the last word, "thanksgivings," into the concept of praying for one another until I realized how Paul prayed. The word in Greek is *eucharistias* and literally means "grateful acknowledgment of God's mercies." Paul's letters glowed with such prayers of thanksgivings, showing his great love for others.

> I do not cease giving thanks for you (Eph. 1:16).
> I thank my God in all my remembrance of you (Phil. 1:3).
> We give thanks to God . . . praying always for you (Col. 1:3).

I thank God . . . as I constantly remember you in my
prayers night and day (2 Tim. 1:3).

I thank my God always, making mention of you in my
prayers (Philem. 4).

I'm encouraged when I learn that I matter enough to
others to occupy their conversation with God. It tells me our
friendship is deep enough to allow us to be open with one
another. It shows me they want to draw alongside my need
(*parakaleo* — remember?).

The prayer-encourager needs three "abilities": vulnerability, dependability, and accountability.

A prayer-encourager's vulnerability

Vulnerability means a heart sensitive to the needs of
others, and a spiritual mindset ready to plead the will of
God. So often people who desire the encouragement and
support of our prayers bleed in silence. Our ears are deaf,
and our eyes blind, to their wounds.

I have a friend who speaks little of her feelings, even
though they run deep and often throb painfully. She told me
her greatest encourager was a girl at Bible college who did
not pressure her to express her hurts but could still sense
them. This friend was so in tune with God that praying for
others floated on the surface of her life. "Sometimes we'd go
jogging," my friend related, "and while we'd run around the
track she'd say, 'Let's pray.' It was so natural for her to do
that."

I see vulnerability too in a friend of Paul named Epaphras.
Writing from his Roman confinement, Paul noted,

Epaphras, who is one of your number, a bondslave of Jesus
Christ, sends you his greetings, always laboring earnestly for
you in his prayers, that you may stand perfect and fully
assured in all the will of God (Col. 4:12).

We hear little more in the New Testament about

Epaphras. Col. 1:7 indicates he had taught the church at Colossae and had come to Rome to see Paul and report on the church's progress. In Philemon 23 Paul calls him "my fellow prisoner in Christ Jesus." Some commentators believe Epaphras was incarcerated with Paul or allowed to become Paul's prison servant.

But why would Epaphras "labor earnestly" in prayer? Doubtless Epaphras told Paul of the heresies troubling the church at Colossae. The congregation needed a corrective and Paul had the clout to deliver it. Unable to visit them in person and straighten them out, Paul wrote a strong letter denouncing their weaknesses. Epaphras prayed that letter to its target, asking God that correction and spiritual growth would result for those at home whom he loved so much.

Intercession for one another, wrote Oswald Chambers, "means that we rouse ourselves up to get the mind of Christ about the one for whom we pray."[31] We can't hurl our requests at God's throne nor dictate to Him what we want Him to do. We shouldn't pray with hearts hardened to His will but that others will discover His sovereignty and His purpose. That's what Epaphras did.

One time a friend phoned and talked of her depression from work conflicts and physical problems. After twenty minutes of it, I noticed myself getting bored and wrapping the cord around my fingers.

Then I felt a prod. The Holy Spirit seemed to say, "Be vulnerable. Pray with her." *Over the phone?* I complained silently. "Why not?" He answered.

As my friend stopped for a micro-second to breathe, I said, "Sue, I don't know what God's answer is for all this, but I want you to know that I care. Before I hang up, let's pray about it."

"Would you?" she asked.

I prayed for God's peace in her life, asking Him to alleviate her pain if possible, to show both of us the reason, and to teach both of us acceptance. When I finished, I heard some sniffling.

"Thanks," she said. "I needed that. It means so much that you would pray. It really helped me see this in another perspective."

One man told of having lunch with a prominent businessman who'd just purchased a large enterprise. Discouragement seeped out of the corners of their talk as the businessman related the weight of responsibility, the slack in business, and unfaithful personnel. He was exhausted physically and emotionally.

The first man admits his first thought was to leave this wealthy friend alone with his problems. But he realized the Bible instructed him to help his friend bear that burden—to be vulnerable (Gal.6:2).

"After lunch we found a quiet spot in his office," he recalls, "and I suggested we have prayer. While I was talking to the Lord on behalf of both of us, this man began to sob. I looked up while praying. Tears were streaming down his face and he was wiping them away with his big rugged hands.

"At the conclusion he said to me: 'Bob, thanks a million. I don't ever remember anyone coming to my office and taking the time to pray with me and for me. This perhaps has been one of the greatest days of my life!' "[32]

Dependability and encouragement prayer

Dependability is the dimension Paul described when he said, "Be on the alert with all perseverence and petition" (Eph. 6:18). The term "be on the alert" comes from one which means being sleepless and watchful. Here it is used metaphorically to suggest that our prayer concern for one another should not be taken casually.

But we often neglect this command. When somebody

asks us to pray for an urgent or pressing need, and we're slightly weary of the whole story, it's easy to say "I'll pray for you" just to terminate the conversation. Besides, it sounds holy. But we often fail to carry through on the promise to pray.

I am shamed over my own failures every time I remember the Lord Jesus' final trip to the Garden of Gethsemane. On that black night before the crucifixion, He singled out Peter, James, and John to stay close while he prayed. "Remain here and keep watch," He asked the threesome (Mark 14:34), then went a stone's throw away and started praying.

You'd think those disciples, after living with Jesus for three years, could read the clues to His distress. You'd think they would have huddled together to pray for Him and with Him. But three times Jesus came back and found them sleeping. In His darkest hours before the cross, His disciples failed Him. He had no support system among His friends. I sense a tinge of pity and remorse in His voice when He asked Peter, "Could you not keep watch for one hour?" (14:37).

He had once reminded His disciples that "at all times they ought to pray and not to lose heart" (Luke 18:1). The King James version says, "faint not." When I read that version I think of a friend's wedding one hot August afternoon when the pastor prayed long and earnestly. Suddenly a loud crash bounced over the pews. I opened my eyes to see the ushers dragging the junior usher out the nearest exit. After he fainted, he wasn't much good at ushering any more! The same for our praying.

But—what results when prayer encouragers are dependable! Many talk about the unbelievable success that Henrietta Mears had as leader of Hollywood Presbyterian Church's college department. Few realize that the woman who preceded her in the post, someone called "Mother Atwood," prayed that department into a powerful instrument of God. Every Sunday morning at five she would be on her knees to pray at least two hours for Miss Mears and the college department. She prayed like that throughout the *thirty-five years* that Miss Mears served at that church.[33]

Paul demonstrated the same persistence. He wrote his son in the faith, Timothy, that he was remembering him in prayer day and night (2 Tim. 1:3). In his commentary on the book of 2 Timothy, Dr. John Stott said he too had a praying spiritual father. Of this man, Stott (a dean of this century's theologians and preachers) remarked:

"I thank God for the man who led me to Christ and for the extraordinary devotion with which he nurtured me in the early years of my Christian life. He wrote to me every day for, I think, seven years. He also prayed for me every day. I believe he still does. I can only begin to guess what I owe, under God, to such a faithful friend and pastor.[34]

For another example of a prayer-encourager, I look to the life of Jim Elliot, martyred along with colleagues by Auca spears in Ecuador in January 1956. Searchers who found their bodies also found Elliot's little black loose-leaf notebook, some of its water-stained pages scattered along the sands of the Curaray beach. He started that little notebook sometime during his first two years at Wheaton College. Its pages held the names of hundreds for whom he had prayed.

A year ago I met a fragile though spritely lady who'd spent many years on the mission field. On a Sunday morning a few months ago a friend found her sitting up in bed, dead. In her lap was her prayer list. What a way to go!

Accountability and the prayer-encourager

Finally, the encouragement of prayer requires *account-ability*.

Over the past few years I've had a handful of friends

whom I felt free to ask to pray with me. I could call or write them, assured they would pray for the answer that would glorify God. They'd also check back to see how God answered.

After one roommate married, she and I met weekly to study Proverbs and to touch base on the parts of our lives we were having trouble yielding to the heavenly Father. We each kept a small three-ring notebook for our Bible study notes, with a couple of blank sheets to mark each other's prayer needs. The left-hand column of those pages was the "date requested" and the right-hand side, "God's answer." Our faith was strengthened as we discerned the ways God was changing us as He answered the difficult prayer needs.

I've also had as a prayer supporter an elderly widow who goes to bed each night to read and pray rather than sleep. I know she prays because she writes (and sometimes calls), reminding me of the specific ways she is praying.

Those on spiritual battlefronts—pastors, missionaries, parachurch workers—say they appreciate most the prayer supporters who want to be accountable.

"One lady told me she remembers to pray for me every morning," one busy pastor told me. "That registers, especially when I have a day when things aren't going as well. Knowing she has prayed encourages me."

My missionary friend Helen says her greatest prayer encourager was a straight-forward woman who meant business when she said, "I want to pray for you." Helen first met this woman as a new Christian in the women's Bible class.

"She was strong and stable," Helen says. "Later when my husband and I went to the field as missionaries, her letters followed us. She'd ask about the Indian people we mentioned in our letters. In other ways, too, she led us to believe she was genuinely interested in our work."

But the woman also sensed Helen and her husband weren't telling her the whole story. After a weekend at that church for missionary meetings, she asked them to breakfast before they left town.

"There were no frills, no pretending," Helen recalls. "She looked straight at me and said, 'Okay, I have a pretty good idea of what you're doing. Tell me what really bothers you out there.'

"At that I was able to open up. I could tell her about my loneliness, my wounded pride in getting behind in the work because I needed to care for my family. All these things we couldn't share in public meetings. So we started a correspondence and I learned I could trust her to pray for the very special needs that we had—the types of things that can't go in prayer letters.

"That woman believed in me and accepted me. To me, she was a picture of the love of Christ, who knows us perfectly and yet loves us anyway."

And when you get right down to the bottom line, being a prayer encourager is simply following the model of the Lord Jesus Christ.

He is vulnerable. "For since He Himself was tempted in that which He has suffered, He is able to come to the aid of those who are tempted" (Heb. 2:18).

He is dependable. "Christ Jesus is He who died, yes, rather who was raised, who is at the right hand of God, who also intercedes for us" (Rom. 8:34). "He always lives to make intercession for them" (Heb. 7:25).

And He is accountable. "For their sakes I sanctify Myself, that they themselves also may be sanctified in truth" (John 17:19).

There is no greater Encourager.

PART III

The Source of Encouragement

Stop, Look, Listen, and Sing 11

Only in the fellowship do we learn to be rightly alone and only in the aloneness do we learn to live rightly in the fellowship. —Bonhoeffer[35]

Discouragement stalked as the young pastor and his wife left town for a vacation with her family in a small town near Beloit, Wisconsin. It was Warren Wiersbe's first pastorate and the church was in a building program—a difficult thing for Wiersbe who couldn't even read a blueprint.

"I was really down and was considering leaving the church and doing something else," he recalls. "One day after we got there I was sunning myself in the back yard. I started to read my pocket New Testament which had Psalms in the back. I don't recall where I started, but the only thing I could see was that David was in trouble. A lot of encouragement that was!

"Then I got to Psalm 33:11—and the Spirit of God just hit me with it! 'The counsel of the Lord standeth for ever, the thoughts of *His heart* to all generations.' God's will comes from God's heart—so why be afraid!

"I can't explain the feeling I had. It must be the way a sail feels when the wind gets into it and it starts to take off. Or the way a drive shaft feels when the power goes on. God gave me new strength and confidence. I went back to the church, we finished the building, and the Lord blessed the ministry.

"To the glory of God, I can say that I rarely have really deep valleys of discouragement," added Dr. Wiersbe, later to become well-known as pastor of Chicago's Moody Church and after that as a teacher with Back to the Bible radio broadcasts. "My personality is more on the optimistic side. But I have always found my encouragement in the Word. I appreciate the help of friends and family, but ultimately it is the Word that sustains me."

The Word and the Spirit

The psalmist said it, too.

Remember the word to Thy servant,
In which Thou hast made me hope.
This is my comfort in my affliction,
That Thy word has revived me (Psalm 119:49-50).

God's Word will give us hope and comfort. And it offers that all the more when we read and study it regularly.

For a long time, I found little encouragement in reading my Bible. I went by the label "Christian" but considered the Bible just some sort of souvenir of the "church part" of my life. As a child I was certainly religious—a pint-size Pharisee who believed the "Holy" part of the title on my little black Sunday book. Once I tripped on the church stairs and my Bible landed in some muddy grass. I was horrified, thinking that meant demerits in heaven.

One January Sunday, to stack up some "spirituality," I resolved to read through the Bible. While my peers did the puzzle in the Sunday school handout, I tuned out the sermon and started at Genesis, chapter one. But the next thing I knew I had woken up.

As I grew up I read portions of the Bible, usually verses assigned for the Sunday school lesson. But it didn't make a lot of sense to me. Short stories in magazines were more my style. I didn't know the Bible had an explanation for my problem:

A natural man does not accept the things of the Spirit of

God; for they are foolishness to him, and he cannot understand them, because they are spiritually appraised (1 Cor.
2:14).

At college a freshman humanities class required that we
read the book of Job in the Old Testament. After that I
figured I'd done my quota of Bible reading for the quarter.
But then I started bumping into people who read the Bible
daily, including the parts I considered obscure and boring,
and talked in glowing terms about it.

More shocks were ahead. A floormate invited me to a
friend's apartment to help her bake a birthday cake. I noticed a list of Bible references posted on the kitchen cupboard.

"What's that for?" I asked.

"Oh, that's for our memory verse review."

I looked again at the list and gasped. The list had fifty Bible verses—references only.

Then another friend invited me to her church. I'd been
going to one like that at home, where we did a lot of stand-
ups and sit-downs and the Scripture reading for the day was
printed on the back of the bulletin. But the people at her
church carried battered Bibles which they marked up during
the sermon! In contrast, mine was so clean and preserved.

Another friend invited me to a dorm Bible study. I encountered more Bible marker-uppers. And I heard about
something called a "quiet time" during which people were
supposed to read the Bible and pray.

Years of church-going had never introduced me to such
practices. All along I thought I'd been a Christian—but here
were people doing things I never linked to the Christian life.
And much involved the Bible.

I took my Bible off the bookshelf (I'd filed it next to Plato)
and began reading in Galatians. I even started marking my
Bible with a red pencil. I didn't like what I read—things like
"a man is not justified by the works of the Law but through

faith in Christ Jesus" (Gal. 2:16).

Then I encountered someone anxious to tell me about a pamphlet called "The Four Spiritual Laws." Law One ("God loves you") was fine with me. But Law Two ("Man is sinful and separated from God") made me squirm.

I began to realize that I was guilty of religious playacting, all worthless to God. He asked, not a sash of merit badges, but an admission that I was a sinner for whom Jesus Christ had died. But I got through college without making that admission. I was too proud.

Finally, one January night a year after college, I realized I couldn't face God in His great holiness if I died. Alone in my bedroom, sensing myself at His throne, I went prone on the floor. "All my righteousness is filthy rags," I whispered. "I need Jesus Christ. Forgive my sins. Come into my life and make me into the person you want me to be."

In silence for several minutes I lay there crying. For years I had winked at God. Now, pride broken, a camel had stooped to enter the eye of a needle.

Over the next few years my Bible reading habits changed from nibbling to devouring. Somebody gave me a Bible in a modern translation and for the first time in my life I read all the way through it. I didn't understand it all, but when I got to Revelation I felt like I had conquered a mountain. Then I started over and was amazed how much of the terrain I'd missed the first time through.

I became one of those fanatics who wrote all over their Bibles. I underlined or asterisked verses that jumped out at me. I drew lines linking key words and phrases. Pieces of a big puzzle started to fit together.

When I had time to myself, my desire was changing from "keeping busy" (biking, baking, sewing) to reading the Bible and praying. Off ink and paper I was sensing the voice of God.

Gradually I was learning what Andrew Murray expressed

in his introduction to *The Secret of Adoration.*

> Take time to read His word as in His presence, that from it
> you may know what He asks of you and what He promises
> you. Let the Word create around you, create within you, a
> holy atmosphere, a holy heavenly light, in which your soul
> will be refreshed and strengthened for the work of daily
> life.[36]

As I read the gospels I was impressed by how much even
the Son of God needed to get away and be quiet. As crowds
pressed more demands on His ministry, Jesus often
withdrew to the wilderness, a mountain, or some other
place alone to pray—to talk with His Father. Sometimes I
can't get over the fact that we have the same privilege as
Jesus—to go right into the Father's presence and ask Him
for encouragement and direction.

Our spiritual survival kit

God has placed in our hands a spiritual survival kit in the
form of a sixty-six-book volume. That survival kit can encourage in two ways. First, it supplies us with God's strength
and consolation. Second, we become messengers of that
encouragement when we can point others to it. It is as Isaiah
wrote:

> The Lord God has given me the tongue of disciples,
> That I may know how to sustain the weary one with a
> word.
> He awakens Me morning by morning,
> He awakens My ear to listen as a disciple (Isa. 50:4).

Bonhoeffer once observed that Scripture study and
prayer are services we owe each other, since through them
we minister to each other. "Because the grace of God is
found in this service," he said, "we should train ourselves to
set apart a regular hour for it, as we do for every other service we perform. This is not 'legalism,' it is orderliness and
fidelity."[37]

The first step in that "orderliness" and "fidelity" is establishing a regular time to meet with God. I've heard many extol the virtues of an early-morning time; I know of others who can meet most peacefully with the Lord at night as they review the day and prepare for the next. Scripture seems to allow both ends of the clock.

> I rise before dawn and cry for help;
> I wait for Thy words.
> My eyes anticipate the night watches,
> That I may meditate on Thy word (Psalm 119:147-48).

I currently do both. I rise at five to catch a bus to work. During that forty-minute trip I review memory verses or read a purse-size New Testament. At night before starting dinner I sit down to meet with God again. I need the refueling for the evening of study ahead.

I know of others who have their appointment with God over lunch hours. Some retreat to their cars as the only private place around. Others, to a library or a park bench. God doesn't care. He just wants us to love Him and to meet with Him.

Then we need to read through His word purposefully. My "method" can be described with the first four letters of the word "devotions"—DEVO. I set aside other time for heavier Bible study, but when I sit down briefly to listen to God I try to:

D—Devour it (immerse myself in the passage);

E—Engrave it (write down in a small notebook something meaningful I learned from the passage. Sometimes that is in the form of a short prayer);

V—Verse it (pick a key verse from the passage; a couple of times a week I put that on a three-by-five card to memorize);

O—Obey it (pray it into my life).

The "V" part, I know, isn't too popular with many people. I've met many who claim, "I'm too old to memorize." Yet when I was a newspaper reporter I interviewed a woman close to ninety who was still memorizing Scripture. She quoted her newest verses to me with a beautiful smile.

The challenge of memorizing

My own Christian growth stagnated until I seriously memorized Scripture, in addition to reading it daily. I began with a course put out by The Navigators which had seventy-two verses. Later, challenged to memorize whole chapters, I started with Romans 8. Little did I know that two years after that, when my mother and father died, I'd hold fast to that chapter's promise that "neither life nor death . . . . can separate us from the love of God." It was as if God knew ahead and wanted to prepare me with His Word.

After Romans 8, God began speaking to me about a pessimistic outlook and so I took on a bigger assignment—the epistle of joy, Philippians. My challenge was a Bible school professor who said he bit off chapters to memorize and devoted fifteen minutes a day to it, using a timer to keep him honest. He even reviewed his verses the morning of his oral exams for his doctorate—when his mind was full of everything else, too.

After that five-month project I concentrated on various Psalms since I wanted the mindset of worship. The message of the Psalms began to get under my skin, and acted as a check whenever my attitudes started to sour.

I'll be honest: I don't memorize easily. My mind is a sieve for names, phone numbers, and dates. In college I had the most creative memory devices on campus for surviving finals. Memorization is plain hard work. I do it by writing out verses on three-by-five cards and reading them over and over, trying to look less each time.

Right now I'm working on the first epistle of John—three verses at a time. One of those verses tells how spiritual growth is linked to God's word: "I have written to you, young men, because you are strong, and the word of God abides in you" (1 John 2:14). God's word will "abide" in us when we read it, memorize it, think and meditate about it, and seek to make it true of our lives.

And we never get to the point where we have enough "Bible." Even Paul wanted to know more. In that lonely letter penned from prison shortly before he was executed, he asked for "the cloak which I left at Troas with Carpus, and the books, especially the parchments" (2 Tim. 4:13). Those were his copies of Scripture!

Jesus Christ set the example for letting the Word "abide" in us. When Satan tempted Him and religious leaders opposed Him, he knew just which passages to quote to disarm them. Satan and his "religious" cronies backed off, defeated by the "sword of the Spirit, which is the Word of God" (Eph. 6:17).

The comfort of Scripture memorized

The enemy that the Word can defeat comes at unexpected times in unpredictable disguises. One man remembers coming home one night from a vacation ahead of his wife and children and found the lights in the house weren't working. Guessing he'd forgotten to pay the power bill, he groped for matches and a candle. At that point he noticed an upholstered chair slashed and the drapes in shreds.

"Candle in hand," he recalls, "I moved from room to room. The farther I went, the worse it got. Great gashes in all the living room furniture. Curtains cut in half. Bedspreads, sheets, and mattresses slashed. My wife's costume jewelry was cut, broken, and dumped into the middle of the floor. An entire rack of ties was cut in half. Suits, dresses, coats and shirts were still neatly on hangers and seemed all right—until I lifted them out of the closets."

Police came and decided juvenile vandals had been at work. He called his insurance agent, only to learn the agent had failed to cover him for burglary or vandalism.

"Alone in the ripped-up, slashed-up house, I went upstairs to go to bed. With my nerves screaming, I turned back the bedspread and sheet in which a huge X had been cut. As soon as I lay down, I felt the rough edges where the mattress had been slit."

Sleep wouldn't come. Finally, he says, "I closed my eyes and, speaking each word aloud slowly, I began repeating Scripture I had memorized: Psalm 1, Psalm 8, Psalm 23, 1 Corinthians 13, John 14, Psalm 46, Psalm 90, Psalm 91, Revelation 1, Psalm 121. . . . I had to go through my repertoire twice, maybe three times. But then I fell asleep and slept soundly till dawn."[38]

I too discovered how memorized Scripture could settle an anxious mind. After my parents' deaths I moved temporarily into their home to begin cleaning it up. Especially at night memories seemed to loom out of every dark corner to renew my grief. I started quoting psalms of consolation and encouragement (such as 139, 121, 46, and 34) which I had memorized in the previous few months. Soon I experienced God's promise: "When you lie down, you will not be afraid; When you lie down, your sleep will be sweet" (Prov. 3:24).

Daytimes, too, during those first difficult months of grief, memorized Scripture verses came alongside like comforting friends. I clung to Psalm 46:1-2a: "God is our refuge and strength, a very present help in trouble. Therefore we will not fear." And I cherished something similar from Psalm 94:18-19:

> When I said, "My foot is slipping,"
> Your love, O Lord, supported me,
> When anxiety was great within me,
> Your consolation brought joy to my soul (NIV).

Thinking through each phrase throughout the day was like clinging to a rock in a storm.

When we receive God's consolation and strength through His Word, we should pass it on. David declared:

> I have not hidden Thy righteousness within my heart;
> I have spoken of Thy faithfulness and Thy salvation.
> I have not concealed Thy lovingkindness and Thy truth
>   from the great congregation (Psalm 40:10).

Telling of God's help glorifies God and is an act of worship.

When I started graduate school after my mother's death, I was uncertain whether I could intellectually (or financially) finish. As my Christian roommate and I talked about these concerns, I told her how Psalm 125:1 hung in my mind: "Those who trust in the Lord are as Mount Zion, which cannot be moved, but abides forever."

She graduated the end of that first term and two years later we got together again. In the meantime she had gone through a difficult job change. "Do you remember sharing Psalm 125:1 with me?" she asked. I had to admit that I had forgotten. "You don't know what that meant to me," she said. "I remembered that promise myself for months afterwards."

The ministry of melody

Another way people have shared their consolation in God's Word is through hymns based on Scriptural truths. The longer I am a Christian, the more I realize why Martin Luther wanted to leave behind a good German Bible and a good German hymnal.

You can't read the Psalms without realizing that praising God goes along with knowing Him. I once tried to count how often "praise" and "sing" appeared in the Psalms, but I gave up the tally. There are too many—verses such as:

> The Lord is my strength and my shield; my heart trusts in

him, and I am helped. My heart leaps for joy and I will give thanks to him in song (Psalm 28:7 NIV).

But I have trusted in Thy loving kindness; My heart shall rejoice in Thy salvation. I will sing to the Lord, Because He has dealt bountifully with me (Psalm 13:5-6).

Great hymns and popular choruses often lift my heart in worship and encourage me. I keep a hymnal near my Bible and study notebook. When I can't sing out loud, at least I can read through the words and sing in my mind.

Sometimes when we're too exhausted or tense to formulate our own prayers, great hymns of the church can become our prayers. Margaret Clarkson, herself the author of many contemporary hymns, remarked, "There is something about the rhyme, rhythm, and musical setting that makes it easier for some people to remember hymns than to recall passages of scriptural prose, and a few lines of verse will often steal into a mind that is too weary to remember much else."[39]

After my parents' deaths, I learned to play guitar. Often, when my grief welled up oppressively, I'd take a break, open a hymnal and play guitar and sing until the despair passed. Lina Sandell's old Swedish hymn, "Day By Day," had many fruitful replays.

Help me then, in every tribulation,
So to trust thy promises, O Lord,
That I lose not faith's sweet consolation,
Offered me within Thy holy word.
Help me, Lord, when toil and trouble meeting,
E'er to take, as from a father's hand,
One by one, the days, the moments fleeting
Till I reach the promised land.

As I continue to include hymns in my private worship time, I find they act like a protective tent over my mind. Sometimes I've woken in the morning with a hymn almost at my lips. When that happens I'm reminded of Psalm 57:8:

"Awake, my glory; awake, harp and lyre, I will awaken the dawn!"

The more I am in God's Word, the more I am encouraged and the more I see victory over a long-term problem: anxiety.

In the spring of 1980 I was so discouraged I was ready to write four-part harmony for the "Broom Tree Blues." My master's degree was in sight but I didn't know if I could meet the deadline looming on my thesis. The job résumés I'd sent out had brought only a trickle of replies—all "no." With the nation's economy getting wobblier daily, I wondered if I'd get any sort of job that made the trials of graduate school worthwhile.

I wondered what I'd do if I had no job by graduation. I was living in college housing and would have to move out when the quarter ended a few weeks away. With my parents dead, I couldn't go home to live with them. All these anxieties had turned into tension headaches which made me feel even worse.

I started slipping out of bed at sunrise to jog away the tensions. One sleepy morning as I walked to the nearby track I noticed the very-awake squirrels racing across the telephone lines to rendezvous at trees. At the track, my feet busy but my mind free, I thought of what I'd just read in Psalm 18:

> For by Thee I can run upon a troop;
> And by my God I can leap over a wall . . . .
> He makes my feet like hinds' feet
> And sets me upon my high places . . . .
> Thou dost enlarge my steps under me,
> And my feet have not slipped (18:29, 33, 36)

Then I remembered those squirrels and their happy high wire act. They had just illustrated it!

In a few weeks—four days before deadline!—I would learn how God had been preparing the right job for me. And I would have a place to live, although "home" for a while would be a borrowed mattress in the corner of somebody's bedroom. But that lonely morning as I circled the track I had the encouragement of the One who guides my feet in frightening places, and who would enable me to scurry like those squirrels.

It was as if my name were written in Scripture.

Just like the story told of a Chinese man named Lo. He had become a Christian and was reading the New Testament in English for the first time. When he came to Matthew 28:20 and read, "Lo, I am with you always," he excitedly pointed it out to a friend and exclaimed, "The Lord Jesus said this just for me—Lo."

Ultimately, he was right.

As the Day Approaches

But according to His promise we are looking for new heavens and a new earth, in which righteousness dwells. —The apostle Peter (2 Pet. 3:13)

Only minutes before, some were dressing for church. Others were pulling comics out of the Sunday paper. Then the giant sleeping beauty awoke with destructive anger that spring day in 1980. A side of Mount St. Helens in Washington state blasted out with a force equal to twenty-five hundred World War II atomic bombs.

The roar resounded two hundred miles away. Trees flattened like match sticks. Ash clouds boiled eastward, burying farming towns in dirty, gritty layers. The heat and force unleashed flood waters and mud slides. Towns were evacuated. Death tolls crept upward—perhaps seventy, some bodies never to be found.

Geologists assessing the situation warned it might be a long time before the volcano, dormant for 123 years, really settled down to nap again. Farmers worried about their crops, thick-dusted with volcanic ash that water turned to sludge.

By coincidence that May 18 I had read Psalm 18, and the news from my home state put real color and noise into verses 7 and 8 of that psalm's imagery.

> Then the earth shook and quaked;
> And the foundations of the mountains were
>   trembling
> And were shaken, because He was angry.

> Smoke went up out of his nostrils,
> And fire from His mouth devoured;
> Coals were kindled by it.

Meantime, in a state at the opposite end of the nation, other tragedies filled the headlines. In Tampa Bay, a freighter struck a bridge support during a storm, tearing away a huge section of the span and causing unsuspecting vehicles to plunge over the edge to their occupants' deaths. Refugees, jammed into small boats, poured into Key West harbors. In Miami, racial riots turned the skyline into a rim of fire.

As always, news from the rest of the world continued to detail war and aggression, famine, drought, floods, poverty, unrest, people crying out in hopelessness.

A man named Habakkuk groaned with similar dismay over the disasters and decline of his times. He complained:

> Why dost Thou make me see iniquity,
> And cause me to look on wickedness?
> Yes, destruction and violence are before me;
> Strife exists and contention arises (Hab. 1:3).

God's answer stunned him. The worst of the worst—the pagan Baylonians—would wipe out his land and people. "God!" Habakkuk cried. "I know my people have rejected You, but this isn't the solution I had in mind!"

Joy in the midst of tragedy

He climbed up in a tower to pout and weep. Finally he acknowledged—as if his farmlands had been buried by volcanic ash and his holdings destroyed by rioters' fire:

> Though the fig tree should not blossom,
> And there be no fruit on the vines,
> Though the yield of the olive should fail,
> And the fields produce no food,
> Though the flock should be cut off from the fold,
> And there be no cattle in the stalls,

> Yet I will exult in the Lord,
> I will rejoice in the God of my salvation (3:17-18).

When everything looked impossible, Habakkuk conceded, the Lord knew what was going on. Even when all material support was withdrawn, he would find fullness of life in God.

Bible expositor G. Campbell Morgan noted that there is something more in Habakkuk's words that doesn't come out in the English translation. "I hope I shall produce no shock when I translate them literally," Morgan wrote. "Take the first Hebrew word [of verse 18] and express it quite literally, and this is it: I will *jump for joy* in the Lord. Take the second of the words and translate it with equal literalness, and this is it: I will *spin around* in the God of my salvation.

"Does that seem as though I were spoiling a great passage? I think some of these passages need spoiling in this way in these preeminently respectable days when congregations are shocked if a man says Amen! Exuberant joy, a bounding joy was this man's experience, and in these words we have such joy expressed. This was no cool, calculating word. I will jump for joy in Jehovah, I will spin around with delight in the God of my salvation."[40]

You need to be tuned to a special wave length to transform disaster into delight. It's easy instead to echo the depression and discouragement of a well-known man who lost his family, livelihood, and health: "My days are swifter than a weaver's shuttle, and come to an end without hope" (Job 7:6).

But God says, "You don't have to think that way."

A living hope

We who live on the A.D. side of the calender—knowing of the victory of the resurrection—can expect that our days will come to an end *with* hope. The Lord Jesus said, "I go to prepare a place for you . . . . I will come again, and receive you to Myself, that where I am, there you may be also" (John 14:2-3). Paul told the Corinthian church,

> Therefore, my beloved brethren, be steadfast,
> immovable, always abounding in the work of the Lord,
> knowing that your toil is not in vain in the Lord
> (1 Cor. 15:58).

And if that's not enough, consider Peter's hymn of hope:

> Blessed be the God and Father of our Lord Jesus
> Christ, who according to His great mercy has
> caused us to be born again to a living hope through
> the resurrection of Jesus Christ from the dead, to
> obtain an inheritance which is imperishable and
> undefiled and will not fade away, reserved in heaven
> for you (1 Pet. 1:3-4).

All around us we may see things withering up. The parched fields of our lives may rasp for the sweet waters of encouragement. But the Lord Jesus has supplied that encouragement. It's called the *future hope*. It's a matchless love story with three chapters titled: "I Love You," "Take Courage," and "I Am Coming!"

I love you

When I read the first letter of the apostle John, I can almost hear the tenderness in his age-graveled voice. "See how great a love the Father has bestowed upon us," he said, "that we should be called children of God; and such we are" (1 John 3:1). The Father loves us and has called us His children—because "in this is love, not that we loved God, but that He loved us, and sent His Son to be the propitiation for our sins" (4:10).

My appreciation of that concept is renewed every time I am on a high place or in an airplane and my view of the world changes from participant to observer. Those big cars, huge lakes, and impassable mountains become mere bugs, mere puddles, and mere crinkles of the landscape. Often I find myself whispering, in prayer, "What is man, that Thou dost take thought of him?" (Psalm 8:4).

Yet the God whose greatness, power, and understanding defy description is also the God who visited this planet to provide a way to show His love in the person of Jesus Christ. Nothing escapes Him. No good, no evil. No rejoicing, no suffering. He is aware of all.

It's our tendency, though, like Habakkuk, to let fearful, discouraging circumstances blot out our vision of a God who loves. But whenever I've allowed that to happen to my thinking, Paul's affirmation of God's character in Romans 8 rings out as an exhortation and encouragement.

> For I am convinced that neither death, nor life,
> nor angels, nor principalities, nor things present, nor
> things to come, nor powers, nor height, nor depth, nor
> any other created thing, shall be able to separate us from
> the love of God, which is in Christ Jesus our Lord (Rom.
> 8:38-39).

I can't think of anything he left out of that list. And when I review it, I naturally backtrack ten verses to another gold-plated description of God's love.

> And we know that God causes all things to work
> together for good to those who love God, to those
> who are called according to His purpose (8:28).

I may not be able to explain everything that happens, but I can never claim He does not love. The verse says, "we know," not "we understand."

David could echo that hope, even though he had plenty of reason to doubt God's goodness. While fleeing mad King Saul, home for David was an assortment of dingy caves. He couldn't go home to his parents or to his wife Michal, Saul's daughter. He never knew who might be a spy to betray his whereabouts. Yet even in those darkest of circumstances, David would affirm:

> I would have despaired unless I had believed that I would

see the goodness of the Lord in the land of the living. Wait for the Lord; be strong, and let your heart take courage; yes, wait for the Lord (Psalm 27:13-14).

Take courage

God's love enabled David to take courage. This was also the message of the Lord Jesus: "In the world you have tribulation but take courage; I have overcome the world" (John 16:33).

The Greek word for "take courage" is *tharseo* and it has been variously translated "be of good cheer," "be encouraged," and "take heart." Jesus gave those comforting words to a paralytic whose friends removed part of a roof to drop him in front of Jesus for healing (Matt. 9:2). He told the same to a desperate woman who had hemorrhaged for twelve years (Matt. 9:22, Luke 8:48). When a storm threatened to swamp the disciples' boat, the "ghost" they saw walking across the waters was Christ who said, "Take courage, it is I; do not be afraid" (Matt. 14:27, Mark 6:50).

Years later Paul sat in prison in Jerusalem, plots on his life thickening after he spoke for Christ before the Pharisees and Sadducees. In the dark discouragement of that cell, "The Lord stood at his side and said, 'Take courage; for as you have solemnly witnessed to My cause at Jerusalem, so you must witness at Rome also' " (Acts 23:11).

Paul had also preached the message to "take courage" to a group of afflicted Christians who wondered whether the Lord would ever come again.

> May our Lord Jesus Christ Himself and God our Father, who loved us and by His grace gave us eternal encouragement and good hope, encourage and strengthen you in every good deed and word (2 Thess. 2:16-17 NIV).

No problem is beyond God's love, but "taking courage" requires our faith—our trust—in His ability to work through us.

I'm reminded of a story told of the English author Thomas Carlyle when he started writing a history of the French Revolution. Like most writers, he wanted a second opinion on his work, so sent the handwritten original of his first volume to John Stuart Mill.

Mill settled into a chair near his fireplace to read the manuscript, fanning the pages on the floor around him. One morning before Mill came to his study, his maid noticed the disarrayed pages on the floor. Thinking them trash, she scooped them into the fire.

Mill was horrified; Carlyle, crushed, vowing never to write again. Then one day Carlyle looked out a window and saw a man building a brick wall. He watched as the man picked up a brick, carefully wedged it in mortar, then picked up another. Brick by brick the wall took shape. He saw the analogy and decided he would write the book again, one page at a time.[41]

He had taken courage—but he had to take that step of faith to start again.

I am coming

At college many of my friends went home nearly every weekend. But my job and heavy study schedule kept me from joining the Friday exodus. It could have been discouraging, except I learned to look forward to quarter's end when I could write home, "I am coming! Can you meet me at the bus station?"

I knew my mom would cook something special. My old bed would have clean sheets. And Daddy would be there at the skid-row bus depot, his fatherly grin a patch of sunshine among the loiterers and derelicts.

After weeks of fish-bowl living, it was a delight to go into "my" room and hear the familiar sounds of "my" home

—not the dorm Juliet on the floor phone with her newest Romeo or three stereos with albums in conflict.

Now, Mom and Dad are gone. That "home" has sold. I miss those roots. But the Lord has reminded me that "if this earthly tent which is our house is torn down, we have a building from God, a house not made with hands, eternal in the heavens" (2 Cor. 5:1).

A few years after the apostle Paul wrote that, his own "earthly tent" was close to being torn down. His pen almost moaned as the weary, doomed man wrote, "I am already being poured out as a drink offering" (2 Tim. 4:6). He could have gone on something like this: "Years and years of serving Jesus Christ and all I get is a stinky prison and nothing to claim as my own."

But that wasn't Paul. His letter to Timothy throbs with loneliness but it also glows with hope.

> In the future there is laid up for me the crown of righteousness, which the Lord, the righteous Judge, will award to me on that day, and not only to me, but also to all who have loved His appearing (v. 8).

At that time the present tense of Paul's life offered no encouragement. But he was certain of the future tense of his life—a new and glorious life with his Redeemer. And that hope permeated his present.

Earlier he had exhorted the Thessalonians not to grieve "as do the rest who have no hope. For if we believe that Jesus died and rose again, even so God will bring with Him those who have fallen asleep in Jesus" (1 Thess. 4:13-14). He told them of the Rapture—that Jesus will descend in great splendor to claim those who are His.

"Therefore," Paul added, "comfort one another with these words" (v. 18). The word "comfort" here is the Greek *parakaleite*—related to that same word meaning to exhort and encourage, gird up and come alongside. He said Christians should encourage one another with the glorious hope of their future with the Lord Jesus. They should remind each other of that other home being prepared in heaven.

Scripture doesn't tell too much about heaven. My mind staggers to understand the symbolic descriptions in Revelation 21 and 22. But I do know one thing. We'll be with Jesus forever. Now we are merely looking in a scratchy, distorted, soot-blackened mirror. Then, we'll see face to face and know fully what we now know only in part (1 Cor. 13:12). That is why Fanny Crosby, blind since childhood, could affirm in her hymn, "Some Day the Silver Cord Will Break,"

> But O, the joy when I shall wake
> Within the palace of the King
> And I shall see Him face to face.

And in another, "To God Be the Glory,"

> Great things He hath taught us,
> Great things He hath done,
> And great our rejoicing through Jesus the Son;
> But purer, and higher, and greater will be
> Our wonder, our transport, when Jesus we see.

Seeing Him—the resurrected Savior—is our future hope, but it is also our present hope for enduring the volcanic disasters and enemy attacks on our earthbound lives. He loves us. He says, "Take courage." We can have, as Paul prayed, "joy and peace in believing" that we "may abound in hope by the power of the Holy Spirit" (Rom. 15:13). And that is also why we are to "hold fast the confession of our hope without wavering, for He who promised is faithful. . . . [Be about] encouraging one another, and all the more, as you see the day drawing near" (Heb. 10:23, 25).

Many have said that this may be the terminal generation. But even if the whole earth does explode like a global volcano, our hope—our faith and His love—will remain.

"For this reason," the soon-to-die apostle Paul wrote, "I also suffer these things, but I am not ashamed; for I know whom I have believed and I am convinced that He is able to guard what I have entrusted to Him until that day" (2 Tim.

1:12).

One early morning I rode a ferry across a part of Puget Sound in Washington state. For those of us on deck the world was a ghostlike mist which chilled our bodies to blueness. Periodically the quiet chill was pierced by the doleful pleading of the ferry horn. It seemed the whole journey would consist of blind nothingness and the steady chug of the boat.

Then, suddenly, we broke through the patch of fog and came into brilliant sunshine. From the air, that fog, which limited our vision and chilled us, probably seemed like a mere cotton ball thrown in abandon on an azure silk sheet. But it had hid from us the warmth of the sun, and the ecstacy of the flawless blue sky.

From the deck we could not see how close we were to knowing the comfort of the brilliant sunshine. From the sky—winging with the gulls—we would have known.

Jesus has told us about the Sunshine ahead for us. And every day, *that* day approaches. That's cause for infinite encouragement.

PART IV
The Results of Encouragement

The Call of a 13
Kindred Spirit

*For I have no one else of kindred spirit who
will genuinely be concerned for your
welfare.* —The apostle Paul (Phil. 2:20)

When I read the newspaper I avoid even glancing at the pollution on the "entertainment page." Yet the book of Judges has some scenes that could outdo Hollywood's worst—from a time when there was no king in Israel, no regard for God, and "every man did what was right in his own eyes" (Judg. 17:6).

One of the goriest episodes comes out of chapters 19 to 21, telling of adultery, perversion, heartlessness, murder, war, and deceit.

We learn about a Levite who went looking for his concubine after she ran away to her father's home. (Times were so bad that a man of the priestly tribe of Levi maintained this adulterous relationship.)

The trip back is what concerns us. They had to stop for the night and by sundown had reached Gibeah, in the territory of the tribe of Benjamin. According to oriental custom, they went to the town square and waited for somebody to offer hospitality. But no one did.

It appeared that they might have to huddle together on a park bench for the night (no motel in those days) when an old man coming in from his field spotted them. This man was from Ephraim—an entirely different tribe and area—but was staying in Gibeah while tending his field. As an outsider, he had no real responsibility for any visitor to the Benjaminite town.

By this time, the Levite was slightly huffy about the cold shoulder he was getting from townspeople. The old man replied, "Peace be to you. Only let me take care of all your needs; however, do not spend the night in the open square" (19:20). The old man knew something the Levite didn't. At night, Gibeah's perverts crawled out of the shadows looking for victims. It was Sodom all over again.

"While they were making merry, behold, the men of the city, certain worthless fellows, surrounded the house, pounding the door; and they spoke to the owner of the house, the old man, saying, 'Bring out the man who came into your house that we may have relations with him'" (19:22).

Not only did the citizens of Gibeah fail to offer hospitality, they wanted to abuse the guest.

The old man's response reminds me of Abraham (who offered Sarah to pagan kings to save his own skin) and Lot (who suggested that Sodom's homosexuals take his daughters instead of his angelic guests). He offered his own unmarried daughter and the Levite's concubine to protect the Levite.

At this point, my reaction is disgust.

But it gets worse. Triple x-rated. In the morning the pitiful, ravaged concubine was found dead at the porch steps.

The plot got bloodier. The Levite chopped her corpse in twelve pieces and sent it throughout Israel as a gruesome call to arms against the tribe of Benjamin. And in the ensuing war, nearly all Benjaminites were killed.

Incredibly thoughtless, all around?

Yes.

Impossible today?

No.

Texts on human behavior often cite the case of a young

woman named Kitty Genovese, repeatedly stabbed on a street corner in Queens, New York, at 3 a.m. one April night in 1964. Thirty-eight of her neighbors watched in silence from behind closed windows and locked doors. They didn't want to get involved. They figured somebody else would help. Nobody did.

Our sin of uninvolvement

Christians often fall in the same shameful league. The sin most churches deny is coldness. People bleeding with emotional and spiritual hurts come in, sit, and leave—unhelped.

Even the apostle Paul knew it was hard to find people with real compassion for others. Under house arrest at Rome, he decided to send a messenger to check on believers he'd left at Philippi. He wanted the encouragement of a good report from them. But the only possible messenger was a young pastor named Timothy.

"I have no one else of kindred spirit who will genuinely be concerned for your welfare," Paul said sadly, "for they all seek after their own interests, not those of Christ Jesus" (Phil. 2:20-21). Except for Timothy there was nobody whose heart beat with Paul's in concern for the brethren he had nurtured. In a way, his moan sounds a little like Elijah—"There's nobody except me left, Lord. Everybody else has gone to Baal."

We need each other

Yet Scripture commands repeatedly that we be of kindred spirit or of like mind. We need each other. As Paul wrote to another church, we need to "encourage one another . . . build up one another . . . admonish the unruly, encourage the fainthearted, help the weak, be patient with all men" (1 Thess. 5:11, 14). We learn compassion by our interdependence. When we cry in close circles, we taste the salt of each other's tears.

The apostle John reminds us that "the one who says he abides in Him ought himself to walk in the same manner as He walked" (1 John 2:6). How did Jesus walk? By reaching out to heal physical, emotional and spiritual hurts. He claimed that He had come to fulfill Isaiah's prophecy.

> The Spirit of the Lord is upon Me,
> Because He anointed Me to preach the Gospel to the poor,
> He has sent Me to proclaim release to the captives,
> And recovery of sight to the blind,
> To set free those who are downtrodden,
> To proclaim the favorable year of the Lord (Isa. 61:1-2, Luke 4:18-19).

Jesus preached the gospel and reached out to the weak and hurting. No less than that did Paul request in his emotion-charged good-bye on the beaches of Miletus.

> In everything I have pointed out to you [by example] that, by working diligently thus we ought to assist the weak, being mindful of the words of the Lord Jesus, how He Himself said, It is more blessed—makes one happier and more to be envied—to give than to receive (Acts 20:35, Amplified).

The community of encouragement

I sense the idea of "the community of encouragement" throughout the New Testament as Christians are admonished to unity in the Christian walk. When we are one in the Spirit, we are to be one in the expression of His love.

What should be the motive for such a "community of encouragement"? In Philippians 2:1-2, Paul suggests four reasons, all signaled by an "if."

> If therefore there is any encouragement in Christ,
> if there is any consolation of love, if there is any
> fellowship of the Spirit, if any affection and
> compassion, make my joy complete by being of the same

mind, maintaining the same love, united in spirit, intent on one purpose.

Paul first notes we have "encouragement in Christ." The word for "encouragement" here is *paraklesis,* again related to *parakletos,* one who comforts, helps, and comes alongside. Through our faith in Jesus Christ, who first came alongside us, we have encouragement.

Next, we have a "consolation of love." Knowing we are loved helps us want to love others.

Third, there is "fellowship in the Spirit." The Holy Spirit draws us together so that our isolationism melts away.

Fourth, we have "affection and compassion." As Spirit-born creatures with God's nature in us, we have the sensitivity and capacity to reach out in tenderness to the hurting.

And with all these "if's" we have a "then"—to be united in mind, spirit, love, and purpose. "Make my joy complete by being this way," Paul said. Then he added, "Do not merely look out for your own personal interests, but also for the interests of others" (Phil. 2:4).

This is the purpose of kindred spirit.

And the amazing thing is that Jesus Christ can use all sorts of materials to create those "kindred spirits." As a contemporary songster has put it, He makes something beautiful out of brokenness and strife.

Matthew put it another way when he pointed out that Christ fulfilled Isaiah's prophecy of One who would not break a bruised reed or extinguish a wick that burns only dimly (Isa. 42:3, Matt. 12:20).

In our days of light bulbs, it's hard to imagine the hope that this imagery of us really presents. But Dr. Kenneth Pike, a world-renowned linguist with Wycliffe Bible Translators and the University of Michigan, helped me understand it when he compared these reeds and wicks to the poor man's candle.

"The Lord takes this figure of the smoking flax," Pike

wrote, "as if, I think, He were in a little American Indian village, such as some I have seen, where the people live in log cabins, or in still poorer shelters. . . .

"In the middle of the night, if these people want to see . . . they find three or four pieces of straw, and they put this straw against a live coal and blow on it until it breaks into flame. As it smokes and burns, a kind of light is made. . . . Christ sees us somewhat like this smoking flax, this burning straw, used as the poorest man's candle."[42]

Christ can use smoky, sputtering, burning straw—imperfect people—to convey His message of light to the world. He will not discard what seems inadequate, because in Him it will be enough. He sees potential in bruised reeds and dim wicks, in people battered and weakened by adversity. He will encourage them—and allow them to encourage others.

And which of us hasn't felt bruised at times?

One woman told how she came home from her graduate internship at a counseling clinic, shattered by a scalding appraisal from her supervisor. As her husband tried helplessly to comfort her, the phone rang. The caller was a woman dying of a terminal disease, who phoned regularly to be comforted and counseled. Reluctantly she went to the phone.

"I'm so depressed," the caller started. "I know you're busy, but I'm so low that I hope you'll talk with me."

"I'm sorry," the woman responded, "but I'm so low myself that I couldn't help anybody."

There was a pause, then the caller said, "I don't know what happened, but I do know this. You help me face reality. You have helped me know what my resources are. And you comfort me."

The woman who had been an encourager was encouraged herself. She put her own depression in perspective and was able to help the caller. One bruised reed to another.

To meet the overwhelming burden of hurting people, a number of Christian psychologists are seeking ways to move the couch into the church and the homes of spiritually mature Christian laymen. One Christian psychologist has even packaged a three-part training program for lay counselors. The first part helps people learn how to express caring to others—in short, how to encourage. The next two training programs help them learn to point failing believers to biblical principles for personal and spiritual problems—in short, how to exhort. This lay "helping" function recognizes both sides of the coin called *"parakletos."*

In some places, "house churches" or "care cells" are springing up to better meet the needs of believers to become accountable for each other for encouragement and exhortation.

But none of this is new. The apostle Paul suggested the prototype when he wrote,

> Blessed be the God and Father of our Lord Jesus Christ, the Father of mercies and God of all comfort; who comforts us in all our affliction so that we may be able to comfort those who are in any affliction with the comfort with which we ourselves are comforted by God (2 Cor. 1:3-4).

When we suffer and are comforted, we are prepared to comfort someone else who now suffers. Our weakness becomes our strength in the community of encouragement.

One minister facilitates this process by plugging persons who've risen above certain problems into the lives of other people starting to go through them. He uses three-by-five cards to record individuals' names and phone numbers and the tragedies they've experienced. Some have struggled against alcoholism, lost a child in an accident, or had financial disaster, unemployment in mid-age, divorce, lingering illness, or a nervous breakdown. But all have been comforted in their affliction and emerged stronger.

When this pastor calls on a person or counsels and discerns that there is a problem similar to that of another member, he asks the hurting individual if he'd like to talk with a person who has struggled successfully. Then he makes a contact and introduces these people.[43]

Many times he has found that those who have been through certain types of problems are much better able to help those still in the midst of these experiences. It makes ministers of his congregation, bringing the church closer to Martin Luther's concept of believers as "Little Christs."

Another pastor had in his congregation a young woman, Janet, who shocked the church on Sunday night by announcing, "I want to withdraw my membership from the church. I have been living a lie, and I can't continue to hide it. Please understand that I appreciate your friendship, and I want to continue as a visitor here. But I have discovered that I don't believe in Christianity as a valid philosophy of life. Therefore I can't remain a member of this church."[44]

She later moved away to Alaska, thinking people would forget her. But they didn't. Cards and letters of encouragement followed her. One young woman named Carole persisted in writing, even though she got no replies from Janet.

When the pastor asked Carole why she kept writing, she replied quietly, "It's just something I want to do. I used to see her in church before, and she looked so lonely I wanted to talk to her, but I didn't know what to say. When she stood up that night, I really felt bad for her. I remember standing up there myself and telling everybody how hard it was for me to accept myself . . . and people showed me they cared. They prayed for me, sent cards, and came to see me. I've never felt so loved. . . . If I could only share some of that love with Janet."[45]

One day Carole received from Janet a note written on a paper torn from a notebook, thanking her for sending a homemade macramé plant hanger. The chink in Janet's armor had been found. She was beginning to understand that somebody really cared.

Two-and-a-half years later Janet returned to town. She

received Christ, was baptized and committed to membership. As she related her story she remarked, "Your love has made God's love real to me."[46] The ministry of encouragement had healed the wound.

Encouragers despite results

But not all stories of encouragement have happy endings. A middle-aged couple who teach a Sunday school class of young single adults find they must often focus their encouragement on those with poor self-images. They encourage many ways—verbal (including phone calls), written (notes), hospitality (lunch dates, outings), and touch—hoping to curb the downward cycle of a poor self-image. "We realize helping these people isn't a one-shot deal," they told me. "It takes a lot of time."

But sometimes nothing they do seems to break through the barriers. They remember one young woman they included in a group invitation to their cabin in the woods. They hoped the outing would give her a different perspective and help her feel part of a warm, loving group. But she was so wrapped up in her problems that she stayed in the cabin to mope instead of accepting an invitation to go hiking and looking for wild flowers.

"When people like that are unwilling to accept affirmation and encouragement," the wife of the couple told me, "I realize I just have to pray for them and for the tearing down of those spiritual strongholds that Paul talked about in 2 Corinthians 10:4-5." And, she added, they've learned they must simply keep on loving, even when that love is unreturned.

That takes us back to our original encourager, Barnabas. He left the results of his encouragement to God. He had no guarantee that his work with Paul or John Mark or any others would pay high dividends. He only knew that he needed to be obedient to the Lord Jesus Christ and express love and concern for the brethren.

In many ways Barnabas was like the nameless little boy who had a lunch bag containing two fish and five loaves of bread. He was in the crowd listening to Jesus preach on the shores of the Sea of Galilee. The four gospels that record this incident say there were five thousand men present. But since Jewish historians failed to include women and children in their tallies, it's possible that there were upwards of ten thousand who had gathered to hear Jesus. And whose stomachs rumbled in chorus as the day closed and they were caught in a wilderness area with no McDonald's handy.

The little boy offered his lunch. Blessed by the Lord Jesus and distributed by amazed disciples, it fed all.

Our lunch boxes may be a letter, a phone call, a smile, a visit, a helping hand, a dinner, a touch, a prayer. They may seem so little in themselves, but under the direction of Jesus they can sustain many. And we'll never run out of people to feed. Just before he died, Dr. F.B. Meyer said that if he had his life to live over again, he would spend much more time in the ministry of comfort and encouragement. Of this J. Oswald Sanders comments: "This ministry of consolation and encouragement is not to be regarded as inferior and of secondary importance. . . . Did we but discern it, we are daily surrounded by lonely, aching and sometimes broken hearts."[47]

Tucked away in the book of Ecclesiastes is a proverb that suggests how we never know what may come of the actions we perform for the sake of the Lord Jesus.

> Cast your bread on the surface of the waters,
> for you will find it after many days (11:1).

Returned in Full

For Joseph Bayly, those many days were "many years,"

yet the bread came back. Many know Bayly, vice president of David C. Cook Publishing Co., as a man of spiritual stature and compassionate depth regarding the Christian response to suffering and death. He has written many books on the subject, including *The Last Thing We Talk About* and *Heaven*, and often speaks in these areas.

It's a ministry rooted in personal struggle. The Baylys have buried three sons: an eighteen-day-old infant; a five-year-old victim of leukemia; and an eighteen-year-old, who had hemophilia complications after a sledding accident.

After the oldest son died, a young woman the son loved and planned to marry sent for the Baylys' comfort a poem written by German pastor Dietrich Bonhoeffer. Titled "New Year, 1945," it had been written by Bonhoeffer for his own fiancée just three months before he was executed by the Nazis at the age of thirty-nine.

The seven-stanza poem, which seemed to speak so directly to the Baylys, included these two stanzas:

Should it be ours to drain the cup of grieving,
even to the dregs of pain, at thy command,
we will not falter, thankfully receiving
all that is given by thy loving hand.

While all the powers of Good aid and attend us
boldly we'll face the future, be it what may.
At even, and at morn, God will befriend us,
and oh, most surely on each new year's day![48]

Several years ago, thirty after Bonhoeffer's death and twelve years after that of the oldest Bayly son, the Baylys received a letter from a young pastor they knew in Massachusetts. The pastor told of visiting over a period of time a woman seriously ill in a Boston hospital. One day the pastor gave her Bayly's book *Heaven*. The next day the woman said she had stayed awake late the previous night to read it. She told of the comfort and help it had brought her. Shortly afterward she died.

The woman had emigrated from Germany shortly after the end of the Second World War. Her name was Maria Von Wedemeyer-Weller. At the time Bonhoeffer was imprisoned and executed, she was the one engaged to marry him.

From Bonhoeffer to Maria. Then from another grieving fiancée to grieving parents. From one of the parents' books to other hurting people. Then, through a friend of the Baylys, back to a dying Maria.

In God's mysterious way, across an ocean and across years, the ministry of encouragement had come full circle. The bread cast on many waters had returned.

God had honored the response of kindred spirits.

Footnotes

1. Dietrich Bonhoeffer, *Life Together,* trans. John Doberstein (New York: Harper & Row, 1954), p.106.
2. Sherwood Wirt and Kersten Beckstrom, eds., *Living Quotations for Christians* (New York: Harper & Row, 1974), p 66.
3. Charles Spurgeon, "Discouragement," *His Magazine* 22, no. 5 (February 1962) : 10.
4. Dr. and Mrs. Howard Taylor, *Hudson Taylor's Spiritual Secret* (London: China Inland Mission, 1950), p. 107.
5. Dorothy C. Briggs, *Your Child's Self-Esteem* (Garden City, N.J.: Doubleday, 1970), p.92.
6. John W. Alexander, *Managing Our Work* rev. ed. (Downers Grove, Ill.: InterVarsity Press, 1975), p. 53.
7. John W. Alexander, *Practical Criticism* (Downers Grove, Ill.: InterVarsity Press, 1976), pp. 20-21.
8. Alfred D. Klausler and John deMott, eds., *The Journalist's Prayer Book* (Minneapolis: Augsburg, 1972), p.59.
9. Donald Bubna, *Building People* (Wheaton, Ill.: Tyndale House, 1978), pp.78-79.
10. Donald Bubna with Sue Multanen, "The Encouragement Card," *Leadership* 1, no. 4 (Fall 1980): 52-53.
11. Taylor, *Hudson Taylor's Spiritual Secret,* p. 107.
12. Bonhoeffer, *Life Together,* p.97.
13. Ibid., pp.98-99.
14. Joseph Bayly, *The Last Thing We Talk About* (London: Scripture Union, 1973), pp.40-41.
15. Keith Miller and Bruce Larson, *The Passionate People* (Waco, Tex.: Word Books, 1979), p.42.
16. Ibid., p.53.
17. Oswald Chambers, *My Utmost for His Highest* (New

York: Dodd, Mead & Co., 1935), p.177.

18. Bonhoeffer, *Life Together,* p. 97.

19. L. Arden Almquist, "Touch: New Dimension of Faith," *Christian Life* (November 1969), pp. 62-63.

20. Bubna, *Building People,* p. 83.

21. "Planting Seeds and Watching Them Grow: An Interview with Dr. Richard C. Halverson," *Leadership,* 1:4 (Fall 1980), p.16.

22. Rick Yohn, *Discover Your Spiritual Gift and Use It* (Wheaton, Ill.: Tyndale House, 1974), p.15.

23. Fred Smith, "Something I Learned from Maxey Jarman," *Leadership* 2, no. 1 (Winter 1981): 93.

24. Ethel May Baldwin and David V. Benson, *Henrietta Mears—And How She Did It* (Glendale, Calif.: Regal Books, 1966), p.172.

25. Wirt and Beckstrom, eds., *Living Quotations for Christians,* p.108.

26. "The Good Seminarians," *Christianity Today* 18, no. 13 (March 29, 1974): 39.

27. Bonhoeffer, *Life Together,* p. 99.

28. Ibid., p.100.

29. Joseph Bayly in "Life and Death: A Symposium," Western Conservative Baptist Seminary, Portland, Ore., February 22-25, 1977, p. 208.

30. Bonhoeffer, *Life Together,* p. 86.

31. Chambers, *My Utmost for His Highest,* p.90.

32. Richard D. Foster, *The Ministry of Encouragement* (Colorado Springs: The Challenge, n.d.), pp.4-5.

33. Baldwin and Benson, *Henrietta Mears—,* p.108.

34. John R.W. Stott, *Guard the Gospel* (Downers Grove, Ill.: InterVarsity Press, 1973), p.29.

35. Bonhoeffer, *Life Together,* p. 77.

36. Quoted in *Hudson Taylor's Spiritual Secret,* p.166.

37. Bonhoeffer, *Life Together,* p.87.

38. Webb Garrison, "The Joy of Memorizing Scripture,"

Christianity Today 11, no. 4 (November 25, 1966): 12-13.

39. Margaret Clarkson, *Grace Grows Best in Winter* (Grand Rapids: Zondervan, 1972), p. 107.
40. G. Campbell Morgan, "Jubilation in Desolation," *The Westminster Pulpit*, vol. 6 (Westwood, N.J.: Fleming H. Revell, n.d.), p. 147.
41. Charles L. Allen, *The Miracle of Hope* (Old Tappan, N.J.: Fleming H. Revell, 1973), pp. 17-18.
42. Kenneth L. Pike, *With Heart and Mind* (Grand Rapids: Eerdmans, 1962), p. 96.
43. Miller and Larson, *The Passionate People*, p. 118.
44. Bubna, *Building People*, p.9.
45. Ibid., p. 24.
46. Ibid., p. 152.
47. J. Oswald Sanders, *People Just Like Us* (Chicago: Moody Press, 1978), p. 169.
48. Dietrich Bonhoeffer, *The Cost of Discipleship,* trans. R.H. Fuller with some revision by Irmgard Booth, rev. ed. (New York: Macmillan, 1959), pp. 16-17.

CHRISTIAN HERALD ASSOCIATION AND ITS MINISTRIES

CHRISTIAN HERALD ASSOCIATION, founded in 1878, publishes The Christian Herald Magazine, one of the leading interdenominational religious monthlies in America. Through its wide circulation, it brings inspiring articles and the latest news of religious developments to many families. From the magazine's pages came the initiative for CHRISTIAN HERALD CHILDREN'S HOME and THE BOWERY MISSION, two individually supported not-for-profit corporations.

CHRISTIAN HERALD CHILDREN'S HOME, established in 1894, is the name for a unique and dynamic ministry to disadvantaged children, offering hope and opportunities which would not otherwise be available for reasons of poverty and neglect. The goal is to develop each child's potential and to demonstrate Christian compassion and understanding to children in need.

Mont Lawn is a permanent camp located in Bushkill, Pennsylvania. It is the focal point of a ministry which provides a healthful "vacation with a purpose" to children who without it would be confined to the streets of the city. Up to 1000 children between the ages of 7 and 11 come to Mont Lawn each year.

Christian Herald Children's Home maintains year-round contact with children by means of an *In-City Youth Ministry*. Central to its philosophy is the belief that only through sustained relationships and demonstrated concern can individual lives be truly enriched. Special emphasis is on individual guidance, spiritual and family counseling and tutoring. This follow-up ministry to inner-city children culminates for many in financial assistance toward higher education and career counseling.

THE BOWERY MISSION, located at 227 Bowery, New York City, has since 1879 been reaching out to the lost men on the Bowery, offering them what could be their last chance to rebuild their lives. Every man is fed, clothed and ministered to. Countless numbers have entered the 90-day residential rehabilitation program at the Bowery Mission. A concentrated ministry of counseling, medical care, nutrition therapy, Bible study and Gospel services awakens a man to spiritual renewal within himself.

These ministries are supported solely by the voluntary contributions of individuals and by legacies and bequests. Contributions are tax deductible. Checks should be made out either to CHRISTIAN HERALD CHILDREN'S HOME or to THE BOWERY MISSION.

Administrative Office: 40 Overlook Drive, Chappaqua, New York 10514
Telephone: (914) 769-9000